Fritos® Pie

NUMBER TWENTY-FOUR:
Tarleton State University
Southwestern Studies in the Humanities

T. Lindsay Baker, General Editor

A list of titles in this series appears at the end of the book.

Kaleta Doolin

Foreword by Davia Nelson

Texas A&M University Press
College Station

Fritos® Pie

Stories, Recipes,
and More

LIBRARY OF CONGRESS CATALOGING-IN-PUBLICATION DATA

Doolin, Kaleta, 1950–
  Fritos pie: stories, recipes, and more / Kaleta Doolin ; foreword by
Davia Nelson. — 1st ed.
     p. cm.
  Includes index.
  ISBN-13: 978-1-60344-256-5 (flexbound : alk. paper)
  ISBN-10: 1-60344-256-1 (flexbound : alk. paper)
  ISBN-13: 978-1-60344-257-2 (e-book)
  ISBN-10: 1-60344-257-X (e-book)
  1. Frito-Lay, Inc.—History—20th century.   2. Frito-Lay, Inc.—
History—21st century.   3. Corn products industry—United
States—History—20th century.   4. Corn products industry—
United States—History—21st century.   5. Family-owned business
enterprises—United States—History—20th century.   6. Family-
owned business enterprises—United States—History—21st
century.   7. Doolin, Charles Elmer, 1903–1959.   8. Doolin, Charles
Elmer, 1903–1959—Family.   9. Corn chips.   10. Cooking (Corn)
I. Title.
HD9049.C8F753   2011
338.7'66475—dc22

2010043205

A ll of this would not have
been possible without these
ingredients: an idea, a converted
potato ricer, courage, determination,
a good product, and the free enterprise
system which has made the Frito
Company a true American
success story.

—*The Fritos Bandwagon*

Contents

Birth of the Frito

A Foreword by Davia Nelson of the Kitchen Sisters

Producers of NPR's *Hidden Kitchens*

I F YOU'RE looking for hidden kitchen stories, Texas is a good place to start. It's a state that's chock full of iconic food with a good story behind it, food that says America. A man with a used potato ricer, some masa, and a dream. It's the stuff our country is made of. We call them kitchen pioneers and visionaries. And Texas in the 1930s was swarming with them. Men, mostly, who dreamed up the 7-Eleven, the Slurpee, the frozen margarita, Dr. Pepper, and the Frito—and changed the way we ate and drank.

We first heard about the birth of the Frito when we were in Dallas gathering stories for our *Hidden Kitchens* series on National Public Radio's *Morning Edition,* a project that chronicles secret, little-known, below-the-radar cooking in America—how communities come together through food. We'd had a long day recording at Fuel City, a palace of a gas station in the shadow of Interstate 30, with twenty-four pumps, a jumping taco stand, a woman selling corn out of a cooler, a herd of longhorns, an oil well, and a swimming pool with bikini-clad pool models. If Hugh Hefner had a gas station, it might look something like this.

Night came. We were strangers in a strange land. Where to eat? A friend had told us to call his pal, Alan Govenar, for advice. Alan is the founder of Documentary Arts, a non-profit organization that champions and chronicles folk and traditional arts through photography, radio, film, festivals, workshops, and new media. Alan invited us over to his archive and walked us through his astounding collection.

When Kaleta Doolin, Alan's wife, joined us for a dinner of barbecue and pie, the four of us were becoming fast friends. We talked about *Hidden Kitchens* and the kinds of Texas kitchen stories we were collecting. After the ribs, we came back to see Kaleta's archive. Kaleta is an artist, filmmaker, community ac-

tivist, and Texan. Around midnight she began to tell us about her family. Her father, it seemed, had invented the Frito: "He was consumed by Fritos. He worked incessantly—at home, on vacation, on weekends. He loved it. He experimented in the kitchen at home. We were his guinea pigs."

"Wait. Stop, don't say another word." We ran and got our mic and machine and she began to tell us her extraordinary American family saga. It was a magical night. We recorded for hours around a big table under low lights and were mesmerized. It was so late, and quiet, and dream-like, with Kaleta's beautiful voice pulling the memories together. It was about two o'clock in the morning when we left.

Kaleta Doolin grew up in Dallas, the daughter of Charles Elmer Doolin, the founder of the Frito Company. Doolin had a bakery in San Antonio, a confectionery. It was 1932. He wanted to have chips on the counter. Tortilla chips staled too easily.

C. E. Doolin was a man of many hidden kitchens. He had the kitchen off to the side of his office. He had a kitchen at home. He had factories, and on a counter in his office, he had a line of Bunsen burners with little tripods with metal trays on top of them. He was always experimenting, mixing up new flavors. He'd call the employees into his office and have them taste the different flavorings for the chips.

There was a secret ingredient in Doolin's Frito. It was his own strain of corn. He had experimental farms where he was hybridizing corn and trying to discover ways to use the by-products. Meanwhile, he and his brother invented a lot of the food-production machinery for the Frito factories, using conveyor belts like Henry Ford did for automobiles. They mechanized the production of snack food. He worked constantly. He had a recording machine in his car to dictate new business ideas and recipes.

Texas of that era was a hotbed of populist thinking. It was a right-to-work state, a can-do kind of place. The East Texas oil fields were discovered in the midst of the Great Depression. There was hope that people could make something out of nothing. C. E. Doolin was part of that spirit.

He also invented Cheetos. He believed in having Fritos and Cheetos as a side dish with a sandwich or a soup. He wasn't consciously making a snack food. He never imagined people would eat a whole bag at a sitting. That was not his vision. Kaleta never brought Fritos to school and didn't have them at home that much. And when they did, her dad brought them off that conveyor belt with no salt on them. Her father was completely committed to health food. He had a bad heart and bad lungs and weight problems. And he was looking for alternative cures. Kaleta was raised vegetarian, and people made fun of her for eating yogurt and figs in her packed lunch.

Mr. Doolin had a restaurant in Disneyland when it was first open, in Frontierland, called "Casa de Fritos." He had a little restaurant in Dallas, also. It was a hybrid of hamburgers and Mexican food. He was on the verge of starting fast food. If he'd lived a little bit longer, McDonald's might be McFrito's or something on that order.

Mrs. Doolin, Kaleta's mother, would use Fritos in cooking, making up her own recipes. Fritoque Pie was one of her inventions. Recipes were printed on the backs of the bags, including our favorite, for making "Jets"—melted dark chocolate covering Fritos, dropped onto a cookie sheet to solidify.

"The Birth of the Frito: A Texas Kitchen Vision" became one of the most popular stories in the *Hidden Kitchens* series. It is the story of a family business, a story that Kaleta had been thinking about telling but never quite had the time or way to bring it all together. We always say most people are sitting on at least one amazing tale. Kaleta Doolin has hundreds yet to be shared.

Something stirred in Kaleta through that telling and the massive reaction the piece inspired on NPR. She was already gathering Frito footage from home movies and the company archives and going in the kitchen and tinkering with the old recipes that were on the backs of the packages of corn chips. The story of the birth of the Frito and her father's relentless vision needed to be gathered and combed. Every time you go to the grocery store you see the legacy of a man who transformed the way America eats. I have wondered, since we did this story for *Hidden Kitchens,* what it would be like to be the daughter of the man who invented the Frito, and the Cheeto as well. A man we consider to be the Thomas Edison of snack food, who could create the mass-produced corn chip in the kitchen laboratory of his own home and develop the clip racks that would display it in grocery store aisles.

Kaleta's quest—through the company archives, interviews with retired employees, her father's meticulous notes, her mother's recipe boxes, her childhood memories—is near to The Kitchen Sisters' hearts. Through the telling of this bit of family history, and delving into it in such a rich and deeply textured way, we know an American family and an icon. A man so full of invention and contradiction.

Fritos were more than a food. They were a community. An old-world way of working: company picnics, contests, Easter egg hunts, celebrations under the trees. It was a company with a vision to weave the corn chip into the fabric of American cooking. From the very corn it hybridized, to the Bunsen-burner experimental kitchens, to the delivery men driving the Frito fleet, to the dieticians it hired to take Fritos as a staple into school cafeteria menus, and to the Frito farms across Texas—it's an endless American story of a man with a pioneering vision, boundless energy, and a genius for branding before the world knew what branding was.

This is a book full of family kitchen secrets and vintage American heirloom recipes. Frito-Ketts, Fritos Chili Pie, Fritos Happy Landings, Fritos Eggplant Casserole, Texas Sombreros, Frito Macaroons, Fritocado Sandwich, Fritoque Pie—all are here to be marveled at and replicated. Cook this book and travel back in time. Peer into the 1950s photograph of the fleet of Frito trucks parading down Houston Street in San Antonio. The long line of big trucks, the marching band, the joyful throng, the sea of straw fedoras. A town gathers in honor of a corn chip whose nationwide success means bounty for all. Kaleta has written a deep-fried, wide-eyed American saga of family and food.

■

Acknowledgments

In my family of origin, I am especially thankful to my paternal grandmother, Daisy Dean Doolin, for inventing the concept of cooking with Fritos; to my father, C. E. Doolin, for his ingenuity; to my mother, Mary Kathryn Doolin, for sharing her precious memories with me; to my oldest brother, Charles W. Doolin, for helping to illuminate our early years; to my older brother, Earl L. Doolin, for saving my life as a child; and to Ronald E. Doolin for allowing me to delve into his past. In my extended family, Alma Ferne Colston helped with Rio Vista recipes and my cousin Colleen J. Doolin Skinner shared stories and recipes from her side of the Doolin family and her information on patent research for all of the Doolin inventions.

As my work moved forward, my wonderful writing coach Mary Allen from Iowa City was invaluable. My writing group, the Forest Lane Writers and Ten @ 10, offered a forum for discussion: Rita Juster, Jane Saginaw, Nancy Allen, Jaina Sanga, Lauren Embrey, Julie Hersh, Trea Yip, Jeanette Brown, Sudeshna Baksi-Lahiri, Donna Wilhelm, Linda Weinberg, and Ann Crow. Several workshop teachers have helped to guide me: Eden Elieff, Kristen van Namen, Beatriz Terrazas, Jennifer Cranfill, and University of Iowa Summer Writing Workshops teachers Mary Allen and Faith Adiele.

This book would not have been possible without the cooperation of PepsiCo, Inc./Frito Lay, Inc., which helped me through all stages of the research and development for this project. I am particularly thankful for the input of Frito Lay retired employees W. Lamar Lovvorn, Ann Lovvorn, Ernestine Putnam, and Helen Harden.

At Texas A&M University Press I truly appreciated the early words of encouragement from editor-in-chief Mary Lenn Dixon. Thom Lemmons, my editor, visited my home and offered astute observations on my research materials. Juliet Dickason provided deep copyediting and recipe suggestions. I am grateful to Pat Haverfield of Haverfield Studios for his expert food photography and to Alan Hatchett for his excellent work in Photoshop on the vintage photos and ephemera.

Most importantly, in my nuclear family I want to thank my husband, Alan Govenar, for his expert writing advice and his support; and last but not least, "thank you" to my stepdaughter Breea and my son Alex for their patience and enthusiasm.

■

Introduction

MY FATHER, Charles Elmer Doolin, was one of four founders of the Frito Company, the company that made and continues to make Fritos® corn chips along with a variety of other snack foods. Charles Elmer (or "C. E.," as he was called) Doolin was also the husband of Mary Kathryn Coleman Doolin, a farm girl fresh out of college with a single year of teaching in a one-room schoolhouse under her belt when they got married. During the Great Depression, my father was a confectioner who made pies and cakes and sold them along with candy and ice cream in his family's store and tiny café. At one point he had to find a way to survive a price war between his ice cream suppliers. His solution was to diversify into other snack foods, including corn chips. As the middle

A 1958 Cooking with Fritos recipe booklet shows some of the recipes developed by Nell Morris. The book is attributed to "Daisy Dean, Fritos Consumer Service." Illustrations were by the Glenn Advertising Agency.

child and first daughter of Charles Elmer and Mary Kathryn Doolin, I've always wanted to know more about my father. He died when I was nine.

After I decided to write a book about my family's story, I wanted to make sure I would have access to research material in the Frito-Lay collection, so I contacted the company. The people at Frito-Lay were very pleased that my book would bring overdue recognition to my dad, and they provided me with my own cubby at their headquarters in Plano (a suburb of Dallas) to do my research. There I looked through boxes of records and min-

Magazine ad used during the Cooking with Fritos advertising campaign, 1950

utes from the early days of the company. I found a huge scrapbook (25 inches by 20 inches, the size of a newspaper "morgue book"), which appeared to be a record of the company's marketing and advertising efforts during the 1950s. The old scrapbook was a treasure trove of old newspaper stories, recipe booklets, recipes clipped from newspapers, food convention programs from the Frito Company's early days, and advertising spreads from *Life* and other magazines. I believe it was put together by Nell Morris, the Frito Company's director of consumer services during the 1950s—her name is handwritten in white ink on its black cover. Looking through that collection, I suddenly knew I had found my compass for writing this book.

Since my family's story is about snack food, fast food, and health food, I decided to make this book a cookbook along with a collection of anecdotes, interviews, childhood memories, and more—in essence, the "world of Fritos according to Kaleta." The book proceeded out of my own research about Dad and his various interests. To find out more about him, I conducted interviews, including some with my mother, read Dad's correspondence, searched the Internet, and listened to old audio recordings dictated by my father. I researched the early history of

Nell Morris, the Frito Company's director of consumer services for more than twenty years, holding court in the Fritos booth at the California Home Economics Convention

The author at fourteen with her first layer cake

the company. I read extensively among the company's early records, watched old films about it, and listened to restored audio recordings. I also searched for reprints of old recipes developed in the Fritos kitchens. Every chapter of this book has recipes at the end, and sprinkled throughout are vintage recipes that I found in that old scrapbook.

I also included my own recipes in continuation of the family tradition of cooking with Fritos. I have never been able to find a meatloaf that tastes like the one my mother used to make, because she always used Fritos as an ingredient in the recipe. When I made a Fritos meatloaf the other day, I told my son that as far as I'm concerned, this is how a meatloaf is supposed to taste: flavorful, with the saltiness and fried corn taste of Fritos replacing the blandness of ordinary extenders and giving the meatloaf a piquant Southwestern flair. As the loaf bakes, it fills the house with the mouthwatering smell of Fritos. (See the recipe for Fritos Texas Loaf at the end of chapter 3, "Frito Kids.")

Cooking with Fritos has become a hobby for me, and I finally realized that I am a third generation Fritos recipe innovator. Cooking with Fritos® must be in my blood.

In chapter 1, "San Antonio," I cover the beginnings of the Frito Company and some other important beginnings. That chapter also discusses how the social atmosphere in the United States during World War II and after it were fertile ground for the success of my father's Frito Company concept.

The author, two hours old, pictured in the company newsletter, the Frito Bandwagon

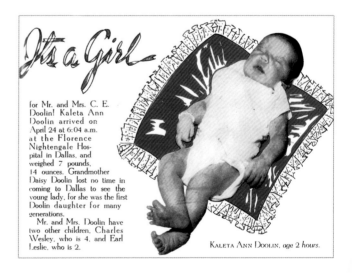

It's a Girl

for Mr. and Mrs. C. E. Doolin! Kaleta Ann Doolin arrived on April 24 at 6:04 a.m. at the Florence Nightengale Hospital in Dallas, and weighed 7 pounds, 14 ounces. Grandmother Daisy Doolin lost no time in coming to Dallas to see the young lady, for she was the first Doolin daughter for many generations.

Mr. and Mrs. Doolin have two other children, Charles Wesley, who is 4, and Earl Leslie, who is 2.

KALETA ANN DOOLIN, age 2 hours.

Frito Recipes
for All Occasions
Distributor - Salesmen, Employees, and all who are interested in good food. These recipe books are available for you and your friends, your customers, and yourself! They are full of grand pepper-uppers for dull meals!
If you want to do something especially nice for your friends, send in their names to the Editor of the Band Wagon, and we will see that they receive this grand book of recipes.
It is expected that distributors and salesmen will send in l-o-n-g lists!
Now that is 1105 Texas Bank Building, Dallas 2, Texas.
Fritos
BOOK OF RECIPES
YOUR FRIENDLY FOOD COMPANION FOR ANY DISH OR DRINK
Anytime Anywhere

Cover of an early Cooking with Fritos campaign recipe book, reproduced for employees in the Bandwagon

Chapter 2 tells about the company's "Cooking with Fritos" marketing campaign, starting in the 1930s, which helped make Fritos a household name. Many of the recipes at the end of that chapter are taken from the menus of two 1930s food conventions, each dish featuring Fritos in every "delicious" bite. Others are recipes Nell Morris developed using Fritos—along with ingredients from other companies whose representatives she made contact with at conventions.

The third chapter, "Frito Kids," covers some Doolin family history and early Frito company history rolled into one. The recipes at the end of chapter 3 were often prepared at our family farm during my childhood, including some recipes for hors d'oeuvre spreads I made as a kid.

Chapter 4, "Diversification," discusses the company's mov-

Mom (right) looking demure with a girlfriend and their horses at the Rio Vista farmhouse

ing into several new areas, including new snack products and canned foods. There is a variety of recipes at the end of the chapter that includes pretzels and potato chips, and some recipes for Tex-Mex dishes that used the company's canned foods.

Chapter 5, "Cattle and Corn," deals with my father's extensive interests, entrepreneurial ventures, and his research in the areas of livestock and agriculture, all of which contributed to the development and success of the Frito Company. At the end of the chapter are several corn-related recipes in honor of my father's agricultural innovations. I've also included some vintage dip recipes and a reconstructed version of the recipe for my father's "sesame crunch" candy.

Chapter 6, "Inventors and Inventions," is about Doolin family innovations, many of which made significant contributions in the food industry. At the end are some recipes developed by my uncle Earl, who was a co-founder of the Frito Company and an inventor in his own right. There are also a few recipes that use jalapeño bean dip.

Chapter 7, "Ronald," is about my Dad's son by his first marriage, who worked in one of Dad's early fast food stands and other places in the company. It also considers my father's—and therefore the company's—forays into fast food chains. From Ronald I learned some choice bits about the early company and about my dad's interactions with his first son, and I also learned that my father was human after all. The recipes at the end of Chapter 7 are related to the company's budding fast food ventures. My father developed some of these recipes himself. There are also a couple of recipes by Ronald.

Chapter 8 tells all about Fritos® Chili Pie—its origins, history, and variations. It establishes that, contrary to an urban legend, the recipe did not come from Santa Fe. The recipes in chapter 8—both my own and others'—reflect the range of possibilities that I uncovered throughout my research into Fritos Pie.

In chapter 9, "Natural Hygiene," I consider my father's avid interest in health food and how that was an important ingredient in the making of the company as well as in the development of Fritos themselves. This chapter also discusses the particular brand of vegetarianism my family practiced when I was a kid. Chapter 9 ends with a group of vintage "health food" recipes, including a number of congealed salads and other types of salad with Fritos as an accompaniment or calling for Fritos to be mixed in just before serving.

In chapter 10, "Desserts," I take you into the kitchen with me and share my childhood memories as I discuss after-dinner favorites we made with Fritos and consider what makes these sweet and salty recipes paradoxically good. This is my favorite group of recipes. Many of them sound crazy, so I had to try them out. It is a chapter full of surprises.

Chapter 11, "Then and Now," brings us up to date with Frito Company history and discusses how the company is moving in a direction I believe my father would have approved of. The recipes (and notes that accompany them) in chapter 11 demonstrate Dad's culinary inventiveness. I've also included here some notes about my own early experimentations with a popular vintage Fritos recipe.

The book's last chapter, "Cooking with Fritos Today," is my chance to shine with my own original recipes. Chapter 12 includes updated recipes with Fritos as an ingredient; I created many of these recipes with the help of Chef Jennifer McKinney and other friends, and some we created separately. The chapter also has notes and comments on how the recipes evolved.

At the end of it all, we come back to the reason I made the long journey through memories and records to write this book: to know, and to honor, my father, C. E. Doolin. ■

Fritos® Pie

QUICK MEAL FOR WINTER APPETITES

Fritos® **Chili Pie**

Chapter 1

San Antonio

ORN CHIPS, which are derived from corn masa like that used in tortillas, were originally developed by Gustavo Olguin. My father worked for him as a fry cook for a short time. Olguin had been a soccer coach in his native Mexico. He and his business partner, whose name doesn't survive, wanted to move back to Mexico, so they sold Gustavo's recipe, his adapted hand-operated potato ricer, and nineteen accounts to my dad. The price was $100. Olguin's business partner loaned twenty dollars to my father (which he soon paid back), and my grandmother hocked her wedding ring for the other eighty dollars. (For a complete account of this transaction see appendix 3, "Letter from C. E. Doolin to the *Frito Bandwagon*." The account was written by my father in 1957 in response to an article proposed by the editor of the *Frito Bandwagon's* twenty-fifth

The larger house, 1416 Roosevelt Avenue, San Antonio, Texas on November 7, 1926 is where Dad lived with his mother, father, and brother when the company started. The smaller house and garage were later annexed for the business. The Model-T was used for deliveries. The photo was taken in the fall of 1926.

▶ The first two chairpersons of the Frito Company—my grandfather, Charles Bernard Doolin, who filled that role for the newly formed company in 1934, and my grandmother, Daisy Dean Stephenson Doolin, who stepped up in 1940 after my grandfather died.

▼ Mother Doolin and her sister Blanche Brawley in their Sunday best. When she was helping Grandmother Doolin with her correspondence, my mother often wrote to Blanche in Gilmer, Texas.

▼▶ Office manager Mary Livingston officiating at a Fritos office party in 1946. She inscribed this photo "To Mother Doolin." The party may have honored Grandmother Doolin in absentia after her first stroke.

anniversary edition. The *Bandwagon* was the company's newsletter for many years, before the computer age.

My paternal grandmother, who eventually became the chair of the Frito Company, was one of its four founders—the other three were my father; his father, Charles Bernard Doolin; and my father's brother, Earl Bernard Doolin. My paternal grandfather died in 1940, six years after the company was chartered. I believe he had a stroke three years before his death and at that point my grandmother inherited the chairmanship from him. Her real name was Daisy Dean Doolin but she was always called "Mother" Doolin by everyone, including the company's employees. She had white sausage curls and wore thick old lady shoes, lilac-scented perfume, and long floral print dresses. She took an active role in the company and was far from being merely a figurehead during her long tenure as chairman of the board.

In 1932 Mother Doolin came up with the first recipe that included Fritos corn chips as an ingredient. Surprisingly, the recipe she invented was a fruitcake. The Doolin family confectionery where Dad worked, Highland Park Confectionery (so named because it was in San Antonio's Highland Park, adjacent to the Highland Park Theatre), had a large poster of a fruitcake on the wall. That might have suggested the idea to her.

It amazes me that through the sense of taste, I can begin

▼ Dad at about twenty (left) with Mr. Armacoast (an employee) and customers in the Highland Park Confectionery. This is where it all began.

Xmas Fruit Cake

There's a new Christmas star in the sky. With the approach of Christmas we are constantly aware of new stars reminding us of The Christmas Story. The Frito Company has a real Christmas Story of its own this year.

All of you by noware aware of the new FRITOS FRUIT CAKE recipe which is being featured in our advertising, on the 29c FRITOS bag, and on the colorful Recipe of the Month cards. Actually this recipe is not a new star, but an old one rekindled by memories.

The FRITOS FRUIT CAKE recipe was one of the original FRITOS recipes developed by Mother Doolin when "Cooking With FRITOS" was in its infancy. The reappearance of this fruit cake recipe of Mother Doolin's will recall other misty memories of early Frito Company Christmases celebrated by Mr. C. E. Doolin and Mr. Earl Doolin at their home in San Antonio.

Too, Mrs. C. E. Doolin will probably be reminded of her college days at San Marcos during the Christmas Season. Mrs. C. E. Doolin, while a student of Home Economics at the college, received a copy of Mother Doolin's fruit cake recipe using FRITOS. She made the cake in conjunction with her home economics work and passed samples around to her classmates at the college.

Mother Doolin's original recipe was turned over to Miss Morris of FRITOS Consumer Service for development into final form. The result—the rekindled star—is the new recipe for FRITOS FRUIT CAKE, another Christmas delicacy.

2	cups sifted flour	3	eggs
½	t. allspice	1	cup pecans
¾	t. cinnamon	¾	cup molasses
¼	t. salt	1	cup blanched almonds
1	cup sugar	2	cups crushed Fritos
½	cup butter	2	Cups mixed candied fruit; lemon
¼	t. soda		and orange peel, pineapple, cherries and citrus

First, sift flour. Add spices and soda. Cream butter and sugar until fluffy. Add eggs and flour, molasses and fruit, nuts and Fritos. Pour into a well greased pan lined with wax paper. Bake at 275° for 1½ hours. Makes two loaf pans.

"Merry Christmas — Happy New Year"

Mother Doolin's fruitcake recipe

to understand my grandmother. I made her fruitcake recipe for our family's holiday celebration this year at Christmastime. With my first taste, I felt as if I could tell what she was thinking when she put Fritos into her fruitcake batter.

The crushed Fritos were included along with candied pineapple, cherries, citron, lemon peel, orange peel, pecans, and blanched almonds. Since she probably baked the fruitcake at the same time the Fritos were made—she, my grandfather, my father, and my uncle made them at night at home, for sale in the confectionary the next day—she probably decided to throw in some broken Fritos to extend the fruitcake batter as well as add nutrition and the flavors of corn, vegetable oil, and salt. It was the Great Depression and it probably felt like a sin to discard good food in the form of fresh but broken Fritos. I can imagine that she was excited about her new idea and that she then began to think of other recipes in her repertoire, like meatloaf and salmon croquettes, which she could also adapt by adding Fritos. After all, Fritos could be substituted for lots of extenders in the same way that bread or crackers or cornbread are used. Fritos could replace cornmeal in batters and be made into breading for salmon croquettes, fried fish, or chicken. She might have begun to think about the possibility that the Frito business could sell more chips if other people became convinced to use Fritos in their own cooking. The company's "Cooking with Fritos" promotional campaign, which began that day in 1932 in Mother Doolin's San Antonio kitchen, grew out of her fruitcake and perhaps other ideas it engendered.

The general atmosphere in the United States at the end of the 1940s and throughout the 1950s was conducive to success for Fritos and the Frito Company. During the 1940s, women were filling in for men, doing their jobs in a national war effort. (At that time, Dad was committed to keeping open the jobs of employees who enlisted or were drafted. "Many of our man-sized jobs have been taken over by the wives of servicemen, and these wives will return to the home with the return of the hero," he said, rather chauvinistically, in a radio interview during the War.) During that time, because so many women were working outside of the home, food manufacturers began marketing time-saving products such as frozen orange juice, Spam, cake mixes, and flavored instant rice mixes. The Frito Company was no exception. One ad campaign during that time said: "Just add

Santa crunching a Frito in a seasonal ad

Cover of an early "Cooking with Fritos" campaign recipe book, reproduced for employees in the Frito Bandwagon

A MONTHLY HANDCLASP BETWEEN FRITO EMPLOYEES

let's start Cooking!

FEBRUARY, 1948

These salmon croquettes are breaded with Fritos.

Fritos . . . and Presto!" The next line said, "Three Easy-to-Fix Recipes!" (The recipes were for Frito tuna salad, Frito loaf, and Frito crackling bread.)

The ad went on to tout the versatility of Fritos: "They're good for breakfast, lunch, snack-time and dinner!" (The recipe for Fritos for breakfast is to serve Fritos with cream.) The ad also told shoppers they could "write the Frito Company for a copy of their big recipe book that gives hundreds of ways to vary your war-time meals."

After the war ended, food manufacturers scrambled to convince shoppers that they still wanted and needed time-saving products—that they still didn't have enough time to use fresh ingredients or make home-cooked meals. Food editors featured the sort of recipes that women were supposed to want, such as "Mock Jambalaya" made with instant rice, canned shrimp, and Vienna sausages, and "Chipped Beef de Luxe" made from chipped beef, olives, white sauce, mayonnaise, and

Employees decorating the Frito truck with flower garlands for the San Antonio parade, April 23, 1947

Frito fleet in the San Antonio Fiesta parade

Here, San Antonio Fiesta parade-goers scramble for nickel bags of Fritos thrown off the back of our trucks.

Angostura Bitters. Women appreciated this continued reprieve from spending hours in the kitchen making things from scratch, according to Laura Shapiro, author of *Something from the Oven: Reinventing Dinner in 1950s America*. In 1960 a popular book came out called *The I Hate to Cook Book*, by Peg Bracken. Commenting on the latter book's title, Shapiro says, "Whether or not [housewives in the 1950s and 1960s] hated making dinner, they did hate the endless silent tyranny of cooking—the pressure to meet its emotional demands and master its technical demands, to accomplish it day after day to the standards set by their mothers, husbands, friends, and every magazine they flipped open."

The Cooking with Fritos campaign took advantage of the general attitude toward cooking among women during the era when Fritos became popular. Fritos made it possible to save time and cut corners. Instead of measuring out cornmeal or flour, oil, and salt, housewives could simply open a bag of Fritos and toss some into the recipe. This was one of several factors that helped Fritos become a staple in virtually every well-stocked pantry in America during the 1950s and 1960s. Fritos also showed up in lunchboxes everywhere, packaged in small stay-fresh bags—because of my father's emphasis on quality control, the Frito Company was constantly updating its bags.

Changes in the way groceries were sold and food was served in restaurants also contributed to Fritos' success. Whereas before the Depression groceries were dispensed from behind the counter, the popularization of supermarkets, starting in the early 1940s, meant customers now helped themselves. Counter-service-style restaurants also started to become popular during the 1940s and 1950s. My father took advantage of these new ways of shopping and dining out by suggesting the idea for the clip rack to the company's engineering department (headed by my Uncle Earl, who, along with Wid Gunderson, a company engineer, patented the clip rack). The clip rack made it possible for customers to get to bags of Fritos quickly and easily. Through personal contact with owners and managers, Fritos salesmen worked at getting Fritos-laden clip racks positioned in snack-food aisles in grocery stores, on countertops by cash registers, in barbecue joints and similar restaurants, and in gas stations (which later developed into convenience stores), where impulse buyers and hungry travelers would see them.

South of the Border

Fritos Mexican Chicken

Green Beans in Butter Sauce
Sliced Pickled Beets
Hard Rolls • Butter
Guacamole Salad (See Page 5)
Lemon Chiffon Pie
Coffee

FRITOS MEXICAN CHICKEN

2½ cups FRITOS corn chips
1 medium onion, chopped
1 clove garlic, minced
1 cup cooked chicken, chopped or sliced
1 cup grated American cheese
1 can (1¼ cups) condensed tomato soup diluted with ½ cup water
1 teaspoon chili powder

Place 2 cups of FRITOS corn chips in a 2-quart casserole. Arrange layers of chopped onion, garlic, chicken and half of grated cheese over the FRITOS corn chips. Pour heated soup with chili powder over ingredients in casserole. Top with remaining FRITOS corn chips and cheese. Bake at 350° F. for 15 to 20 minutes. Makes 6 to 8 servings.

FRITOS CHICKEN A LA KING

6 tablespoons butter or margarine
6 tablespoons flour
½ teaspoon salt
2 cups milk
1½ cups diced cooked chicken
1/3 cup diced cooked celery
3 tablespoons chopped green pepper
2 tablespoons chopped pimiento
½ teaspoon paprika
½ cup diced canned mushrooms (optional)
2 egg yolks
2 tablespoons light cream
3 cups FRITOS corn chips

Make a sauce of butter, flour, salt and milk. Add chicken, celery, green pepper, pimiento, paprika, mushrooms and heat thoroughly. Beat egg yolks and cream together. Add to chicken mixture, stirring for one minute. Serve while hot on FRITOS corn chips. Makes 8 servings.

Regal Fare

Fritos Chicken A La King
Candied Sweet Potatoes
Buttered Biscuits
Spring Salad with Sour Cream Dressing
Fruit Compote
Coffee

A Touch of Texas

Fritos Chili Pie Casserole
Spanish Rice
Mexican Beans
Tossed Green Salad with Tomatoes and Avocado Slices
Oil and Vinegar Dressing
Chilled Pineapple and Orange Fruit Cups
Sugar Cookies
Coffee

FRITOS CHILI PIE CASSEROLE

3 cups FRITOS corn chips
1 large onion, chopped
1 can (2 cups) chili
1 cup grated American cheese

Place 2 cups of FRITOS corn chips in a 2-quart baking dish. Arrange chopped onion and half of grated cheese on top. Pour chili over onion and cheese. Top with remaining FRITOS corn chips and grated cheese. Bake at 350° F. for 15 to 20 minutes. Makes 6 to 8 servings.

GUACAMOLE SALAD GARNISHED WITH FRITOS CORN CHIPS

2 ripe avocados
3 tablespoons onion, minced
1 tablespoon vinegar
1 tablespoon mayonnaise
2 drops hot pepper sauce
½ teaspoon salt
2 tomatoes
1 cup FRITOS corn chips

Peel and mash avocados. Add minced onion, vinegar, hot pepper sauce, mayonnaise and salt. Serve on tomato wedges garnished with FRITOS corn chips. Makes 4 servings.

Monterrey Supper

Guacamole Salad
Fritos Corn Chips
Enchiladas
Tacos
Mexican Beans
Pineapple Whip
Coffee

Sunday Evening

Sliced Baked Chicken • Gravy
Fritos Corn Chip Dressing
Buttered Brussels Sprouts
Cranberry Jelly
Finger Rolls • Butter
Relish Tray — Carrot Strips, Celery Curls, Radish Roses, Sweet Pickle Rings
Baked Date Pudding Ring with Whipped Cream Topping
Coffee

FRITOS CORN CHIP DRESSING

5 slices bread
1 to 1½ cups water
1½ cups lightly crushed FRITOS corn chips (measured after crushing)
½ medium onion, chopped
1/3 cup celery, chopped
½ cup chicken stock
1 teaspoon poultry seasoning
2 teaspoons baking powder
1 egg
1 medium apple, chopped

Soak bread in water until moist. Add remaining ingredients. After mixing thoroughly, stuff bird in usual manner before baking. Giblets and hard-cooked eggs may be added, if desired. Makes 6 to 8 servings.

TUNA SALAD WITH FRITOS

1 7-oz. can tuna
½ cup crushed FRITOS corn chips (measured after crushing)
4 tablespoons green pepper, chopped
4 tablespoons chopped celery
½ teaspoon onion
1/8 teaspoon pepper
Mayonnaise, as desired

Flake tuna, add crushed FRITOS corn chips, green pepper, celery and onion. Mix well with mayonnaise. Serve immediately on lettuce leaf. Garnish with FRITOS corn chips and sliced stuffed olives. Makes 4 servings.

Feed a Foursome

Tuna Salad With Fritos
Broiled Cling Peaches
Cucumber slices
Assorted olives • Celery
Open Toasted Cheese Sandwiches
Raspberry Chiffon Pie
Tea • Coffee

Fritos . . . . FOODS TASTE BETTER WITH FRITOS® CORN CHIPS

4   5

Centerfold of a Fritos recipe book, probably published in the 1950s, including the recipe for Fritos Chili Pie Casserole

Seasonal promotional material used for the cover of the Frito Company in-house trade magazine, September 1956

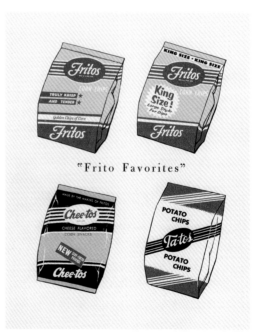

These old-fashioned bags, circa 1954, look a little different than today's.

Display clip racks with rack headers. Small bags of Fritos, Fritatos potato chips, Fluffs (pork rinds), and other Fritos products could be displayed in single, double or quadruple columns, depending on the store's volume.

First Fritos products displayed along with various options for their presentation. Displays like these appeared in grocery stores, gas stations, drug stores, and restaurants. Photos of them helped the retailers choose what they wanted to use.

In his book *Innovation and Entrepreneurship*, Peter Drucker says that changes in any given industry or market structure are an important source of innovation. Industry and market structure can change rapidly, so innovators need to be poised to take advantage of the opportunities that crop up. It's clear to me that one of the keys to my father's success as the head of the Frito Company was his ability to take advantage of opportunities provided by social change. My father was always thinking ahead and always ahead of the curve.

Recipe

Fritos Fruitcake (vintage)

Here's the recipe for Mother Doolin's fruitcake, which probably sparked the idea for the Cooking with Fritos campaign that produced all of the vintage recipes in this book. Nell Morris tweaked this recipe a bit in the 1950s to bring it up to date.

❖ First sift the flour. Add the spices and soda. Cream the butter and sugar until fluffy. Add the eggs and the flour mixture, molasses, fruit, nuts, and corn chips. Pour into two well-greased loaf pans lined with wax paper. Bake at 275 degrees for 1½ hours.

2   cups sifted flour
½   teaspoon allspice
¾   teaspoon cinnamon
¼   teaspoon salt
¼   teaspoon soda
½   cup butter
1   cup sugar
3   eggs
¾   cup molasses
2   cups minced candied fruit: lemon and orange peel, pineapple, cherries, and citrus
1   cup pecans
1   cup blanched almonds
2   cups crushed Fritos corn chips

Chapter 2

Cooking with Fritos

I N 1937 the Frito Company created a point-of-sale department. ("Point of sale" refers to marketing that is used in
stores, such as rack headers and recipe folders; the point-of-
sale department has since been replaced by two departments,
marketing and sales.) The point-of-sale department came up
with the idea for a "Cooking with Fritos" campaign. Or perhaps
Grandmother Doolin came up with the idea when she used Fri-

*Rack headers. I believe the Frito
Company pioneered the use of coined
words and misspellings (as in "krisp") in
advertising as an attention-grabbing
device.*

tos in her fruitcake and in other recipes, and the company just made it official when its campaign began in 1937.

Even before that, in 1935, the company advertised a recipe competition in which cash prizes were awarded for Fritos recipes sent in by members of the general public. That same year, the prize-winning recipes were printed in a recipe booklet, which was available free to anyone who wrote in asking for one. Prize-winning recipes were also dropped into 15-cent bags of Fritos. Sometime in the 1930s, before my parents met and married, my mother was one of the people who submitted a recipe—for Fritoque Pie. (Fritoque is pronounced "Fritokey." In fact, I thought it *was* Fritokey until recently, when I once saw it in print in Nell Morris's collection of newspaper clippings. See chapter 12, "Cooking with Fritos Today," for the recipe, which Mom and I once reconstructed.) For this Mom received one dollar, as did all the other winners of the contest. The

ℱ𝓇𝒾𝓉𝑜𝓈 THANKSGIVING MENU

Pumpkin Soup   FRITOS

Turkey   FRITOS Dressing   Gravy

Fritos Sweet Potato Casserole   Seasoned Green Beans

Celery   Olives   Cranberry Sauce

Rolls   Butter

Fruit Salad in Lime Gelatin

Fritos Mincemeat Whip

Coffee

THANKSGIVING! A happy time for all. At this season, the air is cool, brisk and invigorating lending itself to family and social gatherings.

For this occasion a tasty menu is always the desire of each homemaker, and the success of this festive day depends on how well it is planned and what is on the menu.

All homemakers like to plan their menu around the traditional "turkey" if possible. The menu below may be used on this colorful day with slight variations according to the family's taste.

FRITO DRESSING

3 C. moistened Frito crumbs
1 C. moistened bread crumbs
2 small onions, chopped
3 tbsp. melted butter
½ C. celery, chopped
2 tsp. sage, or more
salt and pepper

Mix moistened Frito crumbs, bread, onions, celery, salt, sage and pepper. Add melted butter and stuff fish, fowl, game or heart.

FRITOS SWEET POTATO CASS-EROLE

1 cup mashed sweet potatoes
1 tablespoon butter
¼ teaspoon cinnamon
¼ cup nuts
½ cup Frito crumbs
8 marshmellows

Mash and season sweet potatoes. Alternate layers and marshmellows. Sprinkle last layer of potatoes with Frito crumbs. Bake at 350 degrees for 2-to 25 minutes. Serves 4.

PUMPKIN SOUP

2 cups light cream (or thin white sauce)
1 cup canned pumpkin
1 tablespoon butter
¼ teaspoon cinnamon
1 dash nutmeg
1 teaspoon salt

Heat cream. Add hot pumpkin and seasoning. Serve immediately.

A Fritos corn chips-laden Thanksgiving menu printed in the Frito Bandwagon, November 1950. *It featured recipes from the company's* Cooking with Fritos *promotional campaign.*

The Fritos corn chip dressing recipe was attached to a rack header next to bags of Fritos in grocery stores. This point-of-sale display was the first of many featuring various recipes with Fritos as an ingredient.

company soon had to abandon the recipe competition because of the overwhelming response.

Some of the recipes sent in by the "housewives of Texas" during the 1935 recipe competition ended up being used by the company over and over in its marketing. In 1950 the prize-winning recipes were appropriated by Nell Morris and, along with other Fritos recipes, given the company's signature label, "by Daisy Dean, Home Economist."

In 1937, the new Fritos point-of-sale advertising department created the first Cooking with Fritos point-of-sale recipe— Fritos Corn Chip Dressing. (See the recipe at the end of this chapter.) The Fritos Corn Chip Dressing recipe was attached to a rack header next to bags of Fritos in grocery stores. This point-of-sale display was the first of many featuring various recipes with Fritos as an ingredient. These displays soon started appearing in grocery stores in Texas and throughout the Southwest. Stores where the displays appeared sold 40 percent more chips than they had before the display campaign began.

The Frito Kid was a regular visitor to grocery store displays. The Kid got passed from store to store by deliverymen according to a schedule.

In 1939 a second booklet containing Fritos recipes was printed and distributed at the State Restaurant Association Convention in San Antonio, where free bags of Fritos were also given out. In 1945 Dad's new office manager, Mary Livingston, in an effort to familiarize herself with all of the aspects of the company, began cooking the Fritos recipes at work. Sometimes she stayed until midnight cooking in the little kitchen next

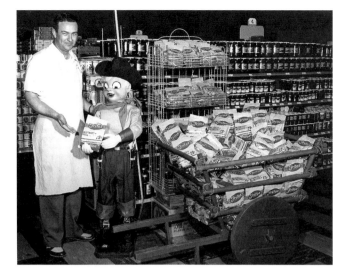

The Frito Kid visits another display.

The Frito Kid strikes again.

to Dad's office (the whole office building was in a converted house). Soon afterwards she went on the road, actively marketing the Cooking with Fritos idea at conventions of food preparation experts—convincing dieticians that Fritos were needed as a staple in the pantry and that they should use Fritos in their cafeteria food. Eventually Cooking with Fritos booths became larger and more widespread at such conventions, popping up

FRITOS

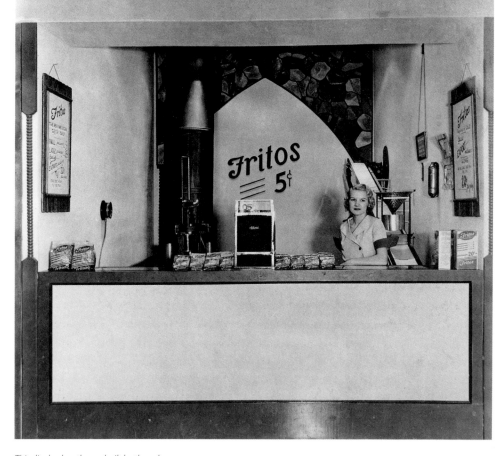

in states as far away as Utah when Fritos' growing distribution made the chips available there. One booth even won an award one year, at the Ohio convention. Along with free Fritos and recipe booklets, recipes that could be used for bulk preparation—featuring ingredients to serve up to 50 people—were eventually given away at the conventions. Participation in various conventions was part of an overall industry trend in which the Frito Company was neither ahead nor behind, as far as I know.

The menu for the 1949 Dallas Dietetic Association Conven-

Sometime in the 1950s this display for distributors showed various company marketing tools. Note the text, "Fritos, the new Mexican crisp chip," printed directly below the emblem boasting "Truly krisp and tender." You can see the clip racks standing in the court-yard and on top of the fence.

tion's closing banquet consisted of Frito-Ketts, Fritos Happy Landings, Fritos Eggplant Casserole, and Frito Chili Pie. I can't imagine enjoying a whole plateful of food with Fritos in every bite. But if you would like to experience the 1949 Dietetic As-sociation dinner, the first four recipes are at the end of this chapter and the last is in chapter 8, "Fritos® Chili Pie."

Another convention, held in 1950 in Washington, D.C., for local newspaper and radio food editors, also featured a dinner menu with four Fritos recipes. The purpose of the convention was two-fold: to promote the use of Fritos as an ingredient, and to introduce a new creation—Cheetos®—which had recently (in 1948) been added to the product line. The recipes served at this convention were Tuna Hors d'Oeuvre à la Frito, Chicken con Fritos, Fritos Fruit Salad Mold, and Fritos-Covered Ice Cream and Fritos Macaroons. Ruth Crane, a radio food critic, said, reporting on the dinner, "The first course was tuna with a touch of onion, pepper, and mayonnaise. The Fritos give just the right texture and taste addition and would be perfect in any kind of seafood salad. The second course was Chicken con Fri-tos, a favorite of the Southwest, where Fritos were introduced. It's a chicken casserole . . . fried chicken in cream gravy with Fritos, tomatoes, carrots, onion, pepper, and seasoning. The salad was a lime gelatin ring mold with chopped fresh fruit in the mold, fresh strawberries in the center and a ring of crisp whole Fritos around the outside. Dessert was a chocolate and

Daisy Dean's Famous **Ten-Minute** *Fritos* Recipes

Nell Morris, a PhD-level home economist, compiled this booklet in the 1950s to promote cooking with Fritos. The character trade name "Daisy Dean" was invented by Nell; it paid homage to my grandmother, Daisy Dean Doolin.

vanilla ice cream mold, rolled in ground Fritos, with a dab of whipped cream and a cherry and Fritos Macaroons. Several of us commented that we'd never thought of using Fritos in so many ways, but I can assure you that we will now." The recipes used to create these dishes are included at the end of this chapter.

In 1950 Nell Morris was hired as the Frito Company's director of Consumer Services. Before that, she had been a professor and dietician at Texas State College for Women, where she was creating bulk recipes using Fritos, cooking the recipes up in her classes, and serving them in the school cafeteria as part of a special arrangement with the Frito Company. She had a PhD in home economics. At that time other companies were using character trade names in their marketing—Betty Crocker was the character trade name for General Mills, for example. Nell Morris may have learned about character trade names during

here's what *Fritos* corn chips **and NESTLÉ's will do to help you!**

1. Furnish FREE special display bins.

2. FREE streamers to be used in dairy cases as shelf talkers and rack streamers. Free Posters.

3. Set up basket displays in your store.

When Nell Morris took over the task of attending food conventions, she began collaborating with representatives of food companies from across the nation and creating recipes using their products in combination with Fritos. Here is an example of material directed to Fritos and Nestlé's distributors in an effort to stimulate sales.

her doctoral studies; it was she who came up with the character trade name Daisy Dean, Home Economist, to attach to Fritos recipes used in the company's marketing. "Daisy Dean" contains my grandmother's first and middle names and was a nod to her inventiveness as the first person to use Fritos as an ingredient.

When Nell Morris took over the task of attending food conventions, she began collaborating with representatives of such companies as Nestlé, Carnation, Pet Milk, and the California

Poster promoting a recording made by the Fritos marketing department in the 1960s. You could order the record by sending 25 cents along with the offer printed on a bag of Fritos.

Foods Research Institute and creating recipes using these companies' products in combination with Fritos. For example, they created the recipe Crispy Semi-Sweet Pie, which uses Fritos in the pie shell and Nestlé's semisweet chocolate morsels and Nescafé in the filling. (The recipe follows.) Nell Morris also developed connections with newspaper food editors at the conventions, to help get Fritos recipes into newspaper food columns.

The Cooking with Fritos campaign waned in the 1970s, perhaps because cooking changed so radically when people started using more gourmet ingredients, in large part due to the efforts of chefs like Julia Child, James Beard, and Alice Waters. Nell Morris retired in 1971 and that probably also contributed to the decline of the campaign. I'm sure that it was discontinued well before the food processor came into use. I believe the common use of the food processor and the proliferation of information on the Internet could bring back the popularity of Fritos as an ingredient in many old and new recipes, since the corn chips can now be made back into a toasted corn-, oil-, salt-flavored masa. ∎

Recipes

The first three recipes were used for the 1949 Dallas Dietetic Association Convention's closing banquet

Frito-Ketts (Fritos' variation on the salmon croquette, vintage)

❖ Crush the corn chips with a rolling pin while they are still in the bag. Prepare 1 cup thick cream sauce (recipe below). Add the flaked salmon or tuna and 1 cup of the Fritos crumbs. Bring to a boil, reduce the heat, and beat in 1 or 2 of the eggs. Cook and stir 1 minute longer and add the seasonings. Spread the mixture in a dish to cool. Then shape it into 2-inch balls and roll them in the remaining Fritos crumbs. Dip into 1 beaten egg diluted with 2 tablespoons water or milk and again in the Fritos crumbs. Fry in deep fat at 390 degrees until light brown. Serve with a sauce made of heated, undiluted tomato or mushroom soup.

THICK CREAM SAUCE

❖ Melt 3 tablespoons butter over low heat; blend in 3 tablespoons flour. Slowly stir in 1 cup scalded milk; season with ½ teaspoon salt and 1/8 teaspoon pepper. Cook and stir constantly until smooth and boiling.

1 bag (8 ounces) Fritos corn chips, crushed
1 cup Thick Cream Sauce (see recipe below)
1 tall can salmon or 1 can (6 ½ ounces) tuna (or substitute 1¼ cups leftover ground cooked meat or poultry)
2 or 3 eggs
1 tablespoon minced parsley
1 tablespoon minced onion
1 teaspoon Worcestershire sauce
2 teaspoons lemon juice
Dash nutmeg
Dash paprika
Salt and pepper to taste
2 tablespoons water or milk
Tomato or mushroom soup, undiluted and heated

1 onion, chopped
1 green pepper, chopped
½ cup chopped celery
2 tablespoons fat
1 bag (4 ounces) Fritos corn
   chips
2 cups tomatoes
⅛ teaspoon pepper
½ teaspoon salt
1 cup grated American cheese

Fritos Happy Landings (vintage)

❖ Sauté the onions, pepper, and celery very lightly in the fat. Add the tomatoes, pepper, and salt and cook 15 minutes. Add the corn chips and mix thoroughly. Fold in the grated cheese, reserving enough to sprinkle generously on top. Place in a hot oven for a few minutes to melt the cheese topping, and serve at once.

1 medium eggplant (about
   1 pound, cut into ¼-inch
   cubes)
2 medium onions, chopped
2 stalks celery, chopped
½ bell pepper, chopped
1 cup tomato sauce or
   tomato soup
½ pound grated American
   cheese
1 small bag Fritos corn chips,
   crushed
½ teaspoon salt
¼ teaspoon pepper

Fritos Eggplant Casserole (vintage)

❖ Peel and chop the eggplant and combine with the onions, celery, and bell pepper. Steam until tender in a small amount of salted water. Mix the sauce or soup, cheese, and some of the Fritos (reserving some for the topping) together and add ⅔ of this mixture to the steamed vegetables. Add the seasonings, mix well, and place in a glass baking dish. Top the casserole with the remaining ⅓ of the cheese-and-vegetable mixture. Sprinkle the remaining crushed Fritos on top and bake at 350 degrees until the cheese is well melted. Serve very hot.
Serves 6–8.

The next four recipes were used for the 1950 Washington, DC, convention. They came from Nell Morris's scrapbook and from the Frito Bandwagon. *(The company took license with its own recipe titles to spice up the convention marketing. Originally, the first three were called "Tuna Salad with Fritos," "Fritos Chicken Dinner," and "Fritos Salad Mold.")*

1 can (7 ounces) tuna
½ cup crushed Fritos corn chips
4 tablespoons chopped green
   pepper
4 tablespoons chopped celery
1 teaspoon minced onion
⅛ teaspoon pepper
   Mayonnaise, as desired
   Lettuce leaves
   Fritos and sliced, stuffed olives
   for a garnish

Tuna Hors d'Oeuvre à la Frito (vintage)

"A rich combination of tuna fish, crushed Fritos, green peppers and celery, a whiff of onion, mayonnaise and pepper," according to radio food critic Ruth Crane. This can be plated to serve four or served on one plate as an appetizer.

❖ Flake the tuna and add the crushed Fritos corn chips, green pepper, celery, onion, and pepper. Mix well with mayonnaise. Serve immediately on lettuce. Garnish with Fritos corn chips and sliced, stuffed olives. Makes 4 servings.

Chicken con Fritos (vintage)

> "A dish that would curl pinfeathers and whet palates"
> —Ruth Crane in an undated Frito Company scrapbook.

In this recipe, you'll cook and bone chicken, make dressing and a sauce, and then combine them before baking.

Once you've prepared the chicken, make the dressing:

FRITOS CORN CHIP DRESSING (vintage)

❖ Soak the bread in water until moist. Add the remaining ingredients and mix thoroughly.

NOW MAKE THE SAUCE:

❖ Combine all the ingredients and cook until thick. Place the dressing in a baking pan, arrange the chicken on top, and pour the sauce over all. Bake at 350 degrees for 1 hour. Makes 8 servings.

2	cups chicken, cooked and boned
5	slices bread
1	to 1½ cups water
1½	cups Fritos corn chips, lightly crushed
1	medium onion, chopped
⅓	cup celery, chopped
½	cup chicken stock
1	teaspoon poultry seasoning
1	egg
2	teaspoons baking powder
1	medium apple, chopped
2½	cups chicken stock
	Salt
5	tablespoons flour

Fritos Fruit Salad Mold (vintage)

❖ Make lime gelatin according to the directions on the package, using the heated orange juice in place of 1 cup hot water. Add the lemon juice and pour into a ring mold. Chill until the gelatin begins to set. Add the pears and pineapple, mix thoroughly, and continue to chill until firm. To serve: Fill the center of the mold with the melon balls and surround the mold with corn chips. This salad is delicious served with a bottled old-fashioned cream dressing, which Heinz still makes.

1	package lime gelatin
1	cup orange juice, heated
1	teaspoon lemon juice
2	cups (total) sliced pears and chopped canned pineapple (or 2 cups of any seasonal fruit or fruit cocktail)
	Melon balls
	Fritos corn chips

Fritos-Covered Ice Cream with Fritos Macaroons (vintage)

According to Ruth Crane, this was a dessert involving chocolate and vanilla ice cream scooped into round balls rolled in ground Fritos, and topped with whipped cream and a cherry, with a Frito Macaroon on the side. According to Nell Morris, "You'll be amazed and pleased at the extra goodness these crunchy corn chips add . . . it's really a delightful surprise."

FRITOS MACAROONS (vintage)

❖ Beat the eggs well and mix with the oatmeal. Let the mixture stand while creaming the shortening and sugar. Combine the two mixtures and add the coconut, corn chips, baking powder, and salt. Drop by spoonfuls into walnut-sized balls and spread on baking sheets. Bake 15 minutes in a 350-degree oven.

2	eggs
¾	cup rolled oatmeal
2	tablespoons shortening
½	cup sugar
⅔	cup coconut
2	cups crushed Fritos corn chips
½	teaspoon baking powder
¼	teaspoon salt

1   package (6 ounces, which makes 1 cup) Nestles Semi-Sweet Chocolate Morsels
¼   cup sugar
1   package (4 ounces) Fritos corn chips, crushed in the bag

1   package (6 ounces, which makes I cup) Nestles Semi-Sweet Chocolate Morsels
2   egg yolks (whites reserved)
2   tablespoons water
2   egg whites, beaten until stiff
2   tablespoons Nescafé
¼   cup sugar
1   cup heavy cream, whipped

Crispy Semi-Sweet Pie (vintage)

❖Put your mold in the refrigerator to chill. Then, make the crust and chill it as well while you prepare the filling:

FRITOS CHOCOLATE CORN CHIP CRUST

❖ Combine and melt the chocolate morsels and the sugar over hot water. Remove from the heat and add the crushed corn chips. Stir to blend. Press on the bottom and sides (not rim) of a 9-inch pie pan. Chill while preparing the filling:
Melt the chocolate morsels over hot water. Beat in one egg yolk at a time until both are fully mixed in. Stir in the 2 table-spoons water until smooth. Beat the egg whites until stiff but not dry and to them add the 2 tablespoons Nescafé. Beat in the sugar until the mixture becomes stiff and appears glossy. Fold the chocolate and whipped cream mixtures into the egg-white mixture being careful to keep as much of the whipped-in air as possible. Pour into the chilled shell. Chill for several hours.

Here's the recipe for Fritos Corn Chip Dressing that was developed as the first Frito Company "point-of-sale" tie-in for the Thanksgiving holidays, 1937.

5   slices bread
1   to 1½ cups water
1½ cups lightly crushed Fritos corn chips
1   medium onion, chopped
⅓   cup chopped celery
½   cup chicken stock
1   teaspoon poultry seasoning
1   egg
2   teaspoons baking powder
1   medium apple, chopped

Fritos Thanksgiving Chicken (vintage)

❖ Soak the bread in water until moist. Add the remaining ingredients, mix thoroughly, and stuff into the bird in the usual manner before baking. Giblets and hard-cooked eggs may be added if desired. Serves 6–8.

Here's a chicken dressing recipe for mass consumption

9   cups crushed Fritos corn chips
30 slices bread, soaked
3   medium onions, chopped
2   cups chopped celery
3   cups chicken stock
3   tablespoons poultry seasoning
6   eggs
4   tablespoons baking powder
6   medium apples
    Giblets (optional)
    Hard-boiled eggs (optional)

Fritos Corn Chip Dressing for 50 (vintage)

❖ Soak the bread in water. Add the remaining ingredients and pour into a greased pan. Bake at 375 degrees for 45 minutes.

The following vintage recipes include Fritos and products made by other companies, such as Pet Milk and Underwood Deviled Ham. These recipes were probably the result of marketing efforts negotiated between Fritos and the various other companies in an effort to sell more of all the products.

Hot Pimiento-Cheese Dip (vintage)

By the Home Economics Department, Pet Milk Company

❖ Put all the ingredients except the pimentos into a 1-quart saucepan. Cook over low heat, stirring now and then, until the cheese melts and the mixture is smooth. Remove the pan from the heat and stir in the pimentos. Serve from a dish placed over hot water or a lighted candle, with crisp crackers or corn chips for dipping. Makes about 2 cups.

   If you prefer a thinner dip, add a few tablespoons of Pet Milk.

⅔ cup Pet Milk
2 cups processed American cheese
2 teaspoons prepared mustard
1 teaspoon Worcestershire sauce
1 teaspoon bottled barbecue sauce
1 can (4 ounces) pimentos, drained and finely cut (about ½ cup)

Fritos Smoke-Flavored Sardine Spread (vintage)

❖ Blend the cheese with the sour cream. Add the olives, seasonings, lemon juice, sardines, and crushed corn chips. Spread on the toasted bread strips.

About 24 finger strips cut from 6 slices of toasted bread

1 package (3 ounces) chive cream cheese, room temperature
1 package (3 ounces) sour cream
2 tablespoons ground or minced ripe olives
¼ teaspoon salt
¼ teaspoon monosodium glutamate (optional)
1 teaspoon lemon juice
8 to 10 smoke-flavored sardines, cut into pieces
3 tablespoons finely crushed Fritos corn chips

Snowcap Spread (vintage)

❖ Combine the deviled ham and minced onion and mound on your prettiest plate. "Frost" with the cream cheese mixed with the sour cream and mustard. Garnish with parsley and serve with Fritos corn chips.

2 cans (4 ½ ounces each) Underwood Deviled Ham
1 tablespoon minced onion (or 1½ teaspoons instant minced onion)
1 package (8 ounces) cream cheese
¼ cup sour cream (or milk)
2½ teaspoons sharp mustard
Parsley for garnish
Fritos corn chips

Ocean Spray's Cranberry-Kitchen Cranberry Burrs (vintage)

❖ Chill the cranberry sauce thoroughly. Make a batter by beating together the cup of flour, salt, milk, and well-beaten eggs. Remove the cranberry sauce from the can in one piece, cut it into six slices, and quarter them. Roll each piece of cranberry sauce in flour, dip it into the batter, and then roll it in the crushed corn chips. Fry in deep fat heated to 390 degrees or in 2 inches of fat in a large skillet (hot enough to brown a cube of bread in 40 seconds). Drain and serve hot with skewered lamb. Makes 24 Cranberry Burrs.

1 can (1 pound) jellied cranberry sauce
Flour for rolling
1 cup all-purpose flour + flour to roll the burrs in
½ teaspoon salt
⅔ cup milk
2 eggs, well beaten
Fritos corn chips, crushed
Fat for frying

Here are a couple of recipes that appeared in newspapers in the 1950s. These recipes also include both Fritos and products from other corporations.

1   pound ground beef
1   teaspoon Accent
1   teaspoon salt
⅛   teaspoon pepper
1   teaspoon chili powder
2   tablespoons butter or margarine
½   cup finely diced celery
¼   cup finely chopped onion
¼   cup finely chopped green pepper
1   can (1 pound) tomatoes
1   can (6 ounces) tomato paste
    Fritos corn chips
½   cup shredded lettuce

Texas Sombreros (vintage)

By Amy Valentine, food editor of the Houston Press, *August 19, 1957*

❖ Break up the meat with a fork in a mixing bowl. Sprinkle the Accent, salt, pepper, and chili powder over it. Toss gently to distribute the seasonings. Melt the butter in a skillet, add the celery, onion, and green pepper and cook until tender, but not brown. Add the beef and cook, breaking it up with a fork, until browned. Stir in the tomatoes and tomato paste and simmer uncovered 30 minutes. Spoon each serving into the center of a circle of corn chips; top each with 2 tablespoons of lettuce. Makes 4 servings.

6   tablespoons butter or margarine
3   tablespoons sugar
¾   cup flour
½   cup crushed Fritos corn chips
½   cup semi-sweet chocolate chips

Valentine Dainties (vintage)

By Eleanor Richey Johnston, Christian Science Monitor, *1958*

❖ Cream the butter and sugar together. Then add the flour, corn chips, and chocolate chips. Mix well. Pat out on a floured board and cut into 12 hearts. Bake on an ungreased cookie sheet at 350 degrees for 12 minutes.

Many vintage Frito recipes were made with avocado. Nell Morris probably collected these from the California Foods Research Institute, which participated in many of the conventions she attended.

2   medium avocados
2   tablespoons lemon juice
½   teaspoon salt
2   tablespoons finely chopped onion
2   packages (3 ounces each) cream cheese
2   tablespoons milk
    King-size Fritos corn chips

Fritos Avocado Cheese Dip (vintage)

❖ Peel and remove the seeds from the avocados; then mash them and add the lemon juice, salt, and onion. Soften the cream cheese with the milk and add to the avocado mixture. Serve as a dip with the corn chips.

Fritocado Sandwich 1 (vintage)

❖ Mash the avocado with a fork and mix with the lemon juice, garlic salt, and crushed corn chips. Use as a sandwich spread.

1 avocado
½ teaspoon garlic salt
¼ cup finely crushed Fritos corn chips

Fritocado Sandwich 2 (vintage)

❖ Mix the corn chips, mayonnaise, and onions together and spread on 4 slices of bread. Broil the ham slices, place them on the Fritos mixture, and top with the other 4 slices of bread. Heat in the oven. Serves 4.

1 cup Fritos corn chips (crushed)
6 tablespoons mayonnaise
¼ cup chopped onions
4 slices ham
8 slices bread

"Calavo," as in the recipes below, is a trade name that combines the words "California" and "avocado." Calavos are extra-large, thin-skinned, bright green avocados.

Salad cream is a dressing similar to mayonnaise but thinner and with a more complex flavor. The vintage recipes below originally called for Carnation Cream Dressing. Nell Morris collaborated with Carnation and other companies to promote cooking with their products. However, Carnation no longer makes the old-fashioned cream dressing, but its competitor, Heinz, still does, so I've made that substitution in the recipe. The salad cream is a little hard to find—I found it in the bulk items restaurant supply aisle at Fiesta.

Calavo Dip with Heinz Salad Cream and Onion Soup (vintage, modified)

❖ Blend the onion soup mix and the salad cream. Let the dip stand at room temperature for at least 15 minutes.

2 Calavo avocados
2½ pints Heinz Salad Cream
1 package Lipton's Onion Soup

VARIATIONS

❖ If smaller amounts are needed, use 1 pint of salad cream and 3 tablespoons onion soup mix.

This is also good as the base for a salad dressing: To ½ cup of the dip, add 1 tablespoon vinegar, 1½ teaspoons sugar, and ½ teaspoon salt.

The dip is also very good when poured on hamburger patties about the last 3 minutes of broiling time.

1 ripe Calavo avocado, cut
lengthwise
½ pint Heinz Salad Cream
Lawry's Seasoning Salt (or
your own favorite seasoning;
I use Murray River pink salt
crystals from Australia)
Doritos tortilla chips or Fritos
corn chips

Calavo Dip with Heinz Salad Cream

(vintage, modified)

❖ Remove the skin from the avocado and save the seed. Mash the avocado with a fork and add it to the cream dressing. Mix well. Sprinkle with the seasoning salt (enough to cover) over the surface of the dip. Mix well. Serve with tortilla chips, corn chips, or the like. To help retain color, put the seed into the dip bowl.

VARIATIONS
I added some lemon juice and water to thin the dressing in the recipe above and used it as a kind of Green Goddess dressing.

1 large Calavo avocado
½ cup sour cream
½ teaspoon salt
1½ teaspoons lemon juice
Dash Tabasco sauce

Calavo Dip (vintage)

By California Foods Research Institute

❖ Cut the avocado into halves and remove the seed and skin. Force the fruit through a sieve. Blend in the remaining ingredients. Makes 1⅓ to 1½ cups.

Chapter 3
Frito Kids

M Y PATERNAL grandparents, Charles Bernard and Daisy Dean Doolin, moved to San Antonio from Kansas City in 1909. They came to Texas because my grandfather's health required warmer weather—he had a lingering illness that may have been tuberculosis—and because they had relatives who lived in Uvalde, Texas, near Big Wells. I've been told my grandmother's parents were opposed to the move.

Eventually, after the Frito Company was established, my father and his brother and parents bought the Rio Vista farm in Big Wells. Big Wells is in Dimmit County in the Winter Garden Region of Texas 60 miles from Uvalde. My mother's father, my Grandpa Coleman, and his second wife, whom everybody always called "Miss Ferne," were hired to be the foreman and book-

After moving from Kansas City, the Doolin family bought and lived in this boarding house at 1416 Roosevelt Avenue in San Antonio. Dad (left) and Uncle Earl are children in this photo, pictured with my grandparents.

▲ *A young Grandpa Coleman sitting on the back steps at the Rio Vista. He was a true Texas cowboy who worked the fields, doctored and fed the cattle, and rode horseback for the roundup before shipping and sales. With Grandpa's help, Dad experimented with cattle feeds and soil conservation as well as with experimental corn and sesame crops.*

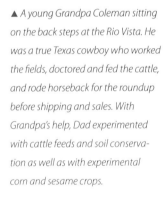

▲▶ *Mom showing dresses she designed and made in her home economics clothing design class*

keeper at the Rio Vista shortly after Dad bought the farm (and before Dad married my mother).

Before he was a rancher, Grandpa Coleman was a baker who owned his own bakery in Three Rivers. During the summers, when my mother was young, she worked in the bakery—she had to stand on a ladder to stir the doughnuts in the hot oil; many years later she told me it was hot and probably dangerous work, the latter because she could have slipped and fallen into the boiling oil. I like to think that my Grandpa Coleman, as a former baker, contributed a piece to my culinary heritage. He was legendary for his generosity. At Easter, he always—with my dad's support—pit-barbecued three goats, set out many cases of candied eggs, and invited the whole county to the farm to celebrate.

The Easter egg hunt was really more an Easter egg grab, because the eggs weren't hidden, they were strewn in a field. The participants gathered at a starting line, Grandpa Coleman fired a pistol into the air (away from the kids, of course), and the participants ran into the field gathering up as many eggs as they could. We went to the Rio Vista every year for the big event and my siblings and I participated in the mad scramble.

Before meeting my father, Mom knew his mother. Mom paid her way through Southwest Texas State Teachers College by

◀ *Grandpa Coleman and helpers (Ed Ackerman) cooking barbecue for the annual Easter party at the Rio Vista. The whole population of Dimmitt County, Texas, was invited.*

◀ *Egg searchers scrambling for Easter eggs sown across a field at the Rio Vista. The Easter egg hunt was really more an Easter egg grab, because the eggs weren't hidden, they were strewn in a field.*

making green salads in the cafeteria. (When I was a kid she told me the salads were so big she had to dive in and use both arms as salad forks to toss them.) She also knitted a vest a week to sell to co-eds and sewed for the college president's wife and for my grandmother Doolin. My mother was an expert seamstress and a very fast knitter; she wasn't left-handed, but she told me that she taught herself a left-handed technique for knitting because it was faster. She also found time to help my paternal grandmother with her correspondence. Grandmother Doolin lived in San Antonio, halfway between Mom's school in San Marcos and her family home in Big Wells, and after she started working for

▲ *Mom as a college girl, sitting in front of a building at Southwest Texas State Teachers College in San Marcos*

▶ *This photo of Mom, hand-tinted by Mom herself in the late 1940s, always sat on Dad's desk at the office.*

Grandmother Doolin, Mom would stay over with her when she was in transit between home and college.

My mom says that her marriage to my father was nearly arranged. He was sixteen years older than she was and they had virtually no courtship. My guess is that Dad probably saw photos of Mom taken at her school modeling the dresses that she made for herself in home economics class, and he fell in love with her finely chiseled nose, blue eyes, perfect skin, and girlish 22-year-old figure. Grandmother Doolin also probably told Dad about how sweet Mom was. I know my parents met at least once before their wedding—perhaps when my father proposed to my mother after getting permission from her father to marry her—because I have a letter he wrote her, dated June 5, 1941, in which he says, "You're such a darling I can hardly wait until

I see you again. . . . The hour is now 12:50 P.M. and I have been interrupted constantly in my work by stealing glances at your darling picture on my desk and calling it sweet names while visualizing the sweet bliss of holding you in my arms."

At the time my parents married, Dad was taking a big step in his life, opening a new plant in Los Angeles; Fritos manufacturing on the West Coast was going so well that he'd had to build a bigger plant. It may have been a period in his life when he was ready for excitement and risk-taking and wanted a partner to share the adventure. Dad wanted to take Mom with him for the new plant's ribbon-cutting ceremony, and because of the social mores of the day, they had to get married to make the trip together. Photos of her taken by my father on their honeymoon show that she was a beautiful but scared young woman.

It was Dad's second marriage. His first wife was Faye Richards, with whom Dad had a son, Ronald, who was ten years old when Mom and Dad married. Ronald boarded at military school and lived with his mom the rest of the time. I interviewed Ronald about his involvement in the early Frito Company and his memories of Dad. (See chapter 7, "Ronald.")

▲ *Ribbon-cutting for the new Angeles plant. From left: George Parker (general manager of the Los Angeles plant), Mary Livingston (office manager), Uncle Earl, and Dad. He and Mom married so they could make the trip to the ceremony together.*

Although my parents' marriage was nearly arranged, I believe they grew to be very much in love. I know my mother mourned my father deeply after he died. He was very dashing with his Clark Gable mustache and Humphrey Bogart hat; she was arrestingly beautiful; and I've always thought they were soul mates. Mom always shopped for him, bringing home multiple suits for him to choose from. (I imagine he almost never set foot inside a retail store. His executive assistant, Mary Livingston, bought his anniversary and birthday gifts for Mom.)

My parents had five children together, three boys and two girls. We were all born two and a half years apart—Mom always called us "stair steps." The timing of our births was accomplished by using the "natural hygiene" (see chapter 9) birth control method, which relied on lactating-related hormone levels to prevent pregnancy; Mom breastfed all of us until we were eighteen months old and then became pregnant after she stopped. (There was a miscarriage between my sister and my youngest brother. He must have been an afterthought, because there are five years between them.) I was the third from the youngest.

My younger sister and I frequently erupted into hair-pulling fights. Mom and Dad expected me to watch her—and my sister expected me to play with her—while all I wanted to do was

Our house on Forest Lane in Dallas the day it was purchased in the late 1940s. The long caliche driveway illustrates our rural beginnings. Eventually the city grew up around us.

◀ There was only a ten-year age difference between Mom and Ronald, Dad's son by his first marriage.

▼ Our family in the early 1950s. From left behind me: Earl, Charles, Dad, Willadean, and Mom. My brother Danny was born later.

▲▲ *Members of the Frito Women's Forum, a group of wives who put on gala company events and invited families of all the employees. Wearing hats to club functions was a sign of the times.*

◄ *Dad acting as emcee at the Fritos Fourth of July party*

► *Thomas Chambers (the porter at the offices of the Frito Company) delivering refreshments at a holiday celebration*

what my older brothers did. I was always challenging the idea that boys should be allowed more freedom than girls. Dad was the disciplinarian, but that didn't prevent me from loving him and watching eagerly for him to drive up the long driveway to the house. I did feel that much of my punishment was unfair. It seemed as if the boys fought and were not punished.

Helen Harden, who started the company's general records department—she was hired to organize Dad's unmanageable filing—and who worked as supervisor of the records department for many years, said, "We had a Dutch door in the entry of our department. One of my favorite memories of your father was of how he would come over after hours when everybody else had gone home. He would lean over that Dutch door, and he'd say, 'Helen, do you have a minute?' Of course I always had a minute for him. And then he'd show me pictures of his kids. Every time he had a child he brought in the picture of the new baby. At the same time he'd show me the latest pictures of the others. Every time I'd see another inch on all the kids."

In recent years I've realized that the early Frito Company was more of a mom-and-pop business than I had originally thought. Mom's position as the chair of the Frito Women's Forum was very significant and helped to define the family-friendly reputation of the company. The Frito Women's Forum was a kind of club for the wives of Frito Company executives and salesmen.

The idea for the Women's Forum with Mom at its head was initiated by John McCarty, director of advertising and public relations, but I believe Dad supported the idea because it gave Mom a chance to feel she had a job in the company and a chance to use her home economics education. Through the Forum, Mom got to know all the other company wives and helped them feel that they were an important part of the company.

The Forum organized events such as company picnics and performances by a children's choir (the children were all offspring of company employees, of course). There were also elaborate holiday events like visits from Santa, western-themed Fourth of July celebrations where the Light Crust Dough Boys performed (I have a photo of my dad as the master of ceremonies at one of these events, wearing a cowboy hat and boots), and huge Easter egg hunts that took up the whole of Reverchon

▲▲ *Celebrating at a Fritos Easter party. I wonder if this food was loaded with Fritos.*

▲ *Mom holding my brother Earl and talking to Billa Willis (the wife of a company employee) at an Easter party. Billa is one of the people I interviewed for this book.*

Park in Dallas. For the latter events Mom had matching dresses designed for herself and my sister and me. The Dallas Easter egg hunt must have been held a few days or perhaps the weekend before Easter, because we also attended Grandpa Coleman's Rio Vista celebration on Easter Sunday. To get to the Rio Vista we had to pack up the car and drive for eight hours.

There were also Christmas parties held every year at Fair Park in Dallas. (This historic park was built in 1936 for the celebration of the Texas Centennial.) At the beginning of the holiday season, Frito salesmen who were "deadheading"—returning with empty trucks to Dallas—would stop at a Christmas-tree farm in East Texas to pick up pine trees for the event. Mom and the other Frito wives made red choir robes with big black snap-on bows for all the Frito kids to wear during the Christmas carol portion of the party. Mom was the chief organizer of all of these celebrations and holiday events, or at least that was the way it looked on the outside. She also gave the other wives hints about home-economics-related subjects and about dress; many of them were from the country and Mom helped them feel equipped for the city life of metropolitan Dallas.

I interviewed Billa Willis, whose husband Bob Willis worked at the Frito Company in Dallas in the 1950s and at Frito-Lay in New York during his later career. Billa belonged to the Women's Forum in 1957. She said, "The Christmas party and the Easter

▲ *Fritatos truck at the Centennial Fairgrounds Fair Park in Dallas*

◄ *Santa greeting guests at the 1951 Frito Company Christmas Party*

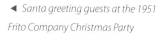

◄ *(L. to R.) Jimmie Pillow, Kitty Doolin, Carrol Doolin, Earl Doolin, and C. E. Doolin at the 1951 Frito Company Christmas Party*

THE FIRST SALES MEETING
FRITO COMPANY OF CALIF.
APRIL 12, 1942

NEWS PICTURES LTD.

▲▲ *Banquet at the end of a national sales meeting in the ballroom in the Adolphus Hotel in Dallas. Mom and Dad are at the head table.*

▲ *California Sales Department Meeting, (this one with wives and children), 1942. Note Mom in her picture hat in the back row next to Dad.*

egg hunt gave us a closeness and a feel of family. Kitty Doolin was a very good example for all the younger wives. She helped us learn to socialize."

I have a picture of my mom standing at the head of a table beside Dad at a sales banquet. She's wearing a dramatic wide-brimmed hat from Lou Lattimore's millinery department. (Lou Lattimore's was an exclusive, high-fashion women's clothing store in Dallas that closed in the 1980s.) All the other women in the photo, seated beside their Frito-salesmen husbands, are also wearing hats. But Mom, standing at the head of the table in her picture hat, is the only one who looks like royalty; she's young, beautiful, and stunningly well dressed. I believe that the company was creating a persona for her, making her a figurehead like the president's first lady, but she was also genuinely involved in the business, developing delivery routes and recipes with Dad.

At the time of my parents' wedding in 1941, the company had a new policy called "store-door," which meant that the company hired its own deliverymen rather than using salesmen who represented other corporations at the same time. This gave the Frito Company complete control over the freshness of its product, since the new Fritos deliverymen stocked the store shelves themselves and removed any out-of-date product.

The business's expansion into the West Coast market made the new store policy feasible financially. Mom helped Dad figure out store-door delivery routes by stringing yarn along a map onto pins stuck into the carpet of their temporary home in Los Angeles when they were there on their honeymoon.

Frito sales meeting at the California office

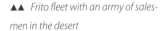

▲▲ *Frito fleet with an army of sales-men in the desert*

◀ *Early company treasurer Emile Jurica standing with Eugene Davis (who designed and engineered the company's early plants)*

▶ *Dad was really proud of Fritos' sales force and their trucks.*

Later on Mom supported company entertaining at home. Emil Jurica, the company treasurer, always showed up in his little round wire-rimmed glasses and his spats, which made an indelible impression on me. Before that I had only seen spats in old silent movies; Mr. Jurica was the only person I ever saw wearing them as part of his normal attire. There was also an architect, Eugene Davis, who was a regular off-hours visitor. During one of his visits to the house, Mr. Davis brought us a tiny box of sharks' teeth and shell fossils and taught my brothers and sister and me about fossils. We were totally fascinated by the teeth and fossils, taking them out one by one, turning them over and over, and memorizing the way they looked. Later, Mom and Dad decided to buy a load of shell gravel to mix with cement to pave our driveway, and my sister and I had endless fun hunting in it for the fossils we had learned about from Mr. Davis, telling ourselves we were looking for

The company gas station that served Fritos delivery trucks. The gas pumps display the famous Fritos emblem.

diamonds. The gravel was from the bottom of a river and we found many shells and sharks' teeth in it. I was so impressed by all of this that when I was older I considered becoming an archaeologist.

Mr. Davis was the architect of all the various parts of the Frito plant in Dallas. The plant included the company's grain elevator, where all the corn was stored; the machine shop (which my Uncle Earl was in charge of); the food processing area; and the shipping warehouse, all built by Mr. Davis in 1947. The grain elevator was an engineering feat involving a continuous concrete pour. The plant's new location was next to the railroad tracks and close to Fair Park, and I've been told by someone who lived in a nearby area called Freedman's Town (where many freed slaves originally settled after emancipation in Texas) that the smell of frying corn and potato chips from the plant was tantalizing to everyone attending the fair. I imagine that Mr. Davis and Dad became very close during those early years of the company's growth. Mr. Davis must have known a lot about Dad's goals for the future. All I know about their meetings is that their discussions were very long and that Mr. Davis was always carrying a set of rolled-up plans.

The amount of time Dad gave to his company was phenomenal. It seems that everything he did (except, of course, for creating us) was related to the business. Our life experiences were very different from anyone else's. The company had a televised advertising campaign in the 1950s that featured a character named the Frito Kid. He was a little cowboy who rustled up grub—that is, Fritos—with a lasso and said things like, "Howdy, Partner." I often thought of us as the real Frito Kids. My siblings and I were very indoctrinated in the business, learning about different aspects of it in all of our time and travels with Dad.

When I was young we often visited the Rio Vista Farm. Hunting and fishing at the Rio Vista were used as "perks" for employees and relatives, although I didn't realize that when I was a child. Grandpa Coleman's family was basically running a hunting camp, where white-tail deer, doves, rabbits, quail, wild boars, and wild turkeys were abundant. There were tractors and plows and trucks galore on the farm. Mom's half-brothers, who grew up on the ranch, told me that Dad showed them how to organize the parts of a tractor that was being repaired, to be

This is a chip-sorting machine prototype, shown with Dad (center), company architect Eugene Davis, and Uncle Earl. This photo was taken for the employees to see the progress of the company through the documentation presented in the Bandwagon.

Cover of the Frito Bandwagon *June 1955 issue, which highlighted the Casa de Fritos venture at Disneyland*

better able to reassemble it. I never got to know the "masculine" trades that Dad taught the boys, but I did learn to love tools.

Meal preparation was a group activity that all of the women participated in while the men hunted. I learned to spread peanut butter and jelly or pimento cheese on white bread, and mayonnaise on bologna sandwiches. Only while we were at the Rio Vista were my brothers and sister and I allowed to eat white bread; we always had whole wheat or seven grain at home. I also prepared sandwiches with meat spread (see the recipe at the end of this chapter) made by my grandfather's second wife, Miss Ferne, and I watched Miss Ferne prepare biscuits, enchiladas, tamales, eggs, venison, quail, dove, chicken, and rabbit. I also learned how to pluck a chicken.

Everyone always called my grandfather's wife "Miss Ferne," including my grandfather, who had known her by that name before they were married. Grandpa had married Miss Ferne in the 1930s after his first wife (my maternal grandmother) died from blood poisoning. Miss Ferne was only ten years older than my mother; in fact, she and Mom attended school together in Big Wells. Miss Ferne always wore an apron, whether she was cooking dinner or feeding or plucking and butchering chickens; her hair was always permed, and with her weathered face she never looked young to me. We were at the New York World's Fair when we were called back to Texas for my grandfather's funeral in 1964. Miss Ferne died at the age of 96; she retained a sharp mind and a clear memory right up until her death.

At the Rio Vista every year at Christmastime, my mother, my sister, and I, Miss Ferne and her three daughters, and two women friends from Big Wells—Olivia Martinez and her mother—made many dozens of tamales at a party called the Tamalada. Afterwards we divided up the tamales to put in our various freezers and give as gifts. In Miss Ferne's records, I found a picture of Olivia Martinez; she appears to be in her mid-twenties and is movie-star beautiful. I remember that during the Tamalada the kitchen was filled with laughter and with the smells of chili pepper, cumin, garlic, boiling brisket, and steaming corn masa. I can still hear the Texas twangs punctuated with Mexican exclamations. To experience the spirit of a Tamalada, you (and a group of friends of family members) should make a bulk recipe for beef brisket tamales that I learned from Irma Gonzales

▲ *There were tractors and plows and trucks galore on the Rio Vista farm.*

◄ *Mom with her parents and siblings, circa 1940. From left: Ruby Lea and Pauline (Mom's full sisters), Mom, Miss Ferne, Grandpa Coleman, and Daisy (Mom's oldest half sister).*

Flores, the head chef at the Wesley Rankin Community Center of Dallas (see page 164).

Because of his weak heart, Dad always preferred to travel by train or car. We often traveled as a family from Dallas to Los Angeles, where we visited Grandmother Doolin's relatives and where a part of Dad's work was located. Our vehicles were company-owned cars in which we were overcrowded, one of us sharing the front seat with Mom and Dad and three of us in the back. A few times we even took along some extra relatives, who also sat crammed into the back seat. I learned to dread those trips, especially the long hot stretches through the desert. My brother Earl remembers that on one of our trips, I almost fell out of the car while Dad was driving through the desert. I was claustrophobic from once getting trapped in an icebox, so I'm sure I was hanging out the backseat window to get some air. Earl caught me by my heels and was holding on for dear life when Dad turned around in the driver's seat and, not knowing the circumstances, thumped him on the head. Dad's way of dealing with rowdy kids in close quarters while he was driving was to turn around and deliver a quick thump. Earl says that he had a furious need to rub his head, but he held on to me instead.

"I wonder if my ocean will still be there," I said once as we neared our first glimpse of the water, at the end of one of those long road trips to California. I was five at the time. Everyone laughed, and I'm teased by my family about the comment to this day. We always had a wonderful, magical, exciting time in California. Even visiting relatives was fun. We swam in the Hotel Miramar pool with Patty McCormick, the child star of *The Wild Seed,* and we were inducted into the honorary Mouseketeers by "Uncle Roy" (Walt Disney's brother and the host of the Mickey Mouse Club), after we got to meet "Uncle Walt" himself. Being at the beach meant hours and hours of fun, at least as much fun as we could possibly have with our governess, Verna Johnson, watching us.

Dad had to work at the office every day, so we played and went sightseeing with Mom. The botanical gardens became so familiar that they seemed like an old friend when I revisited them in my married life. Mom loved taking jillions of pictures of us smelling flowers. The flower-sniffing occurred at her insistence, because she was always trying to add a little interest

to her snapshots. We also visited Dad at work and were paraded around the factory to meet all the employees. I imagined myself as royalty performing a "white glove test," but my brothers and sister and I were really more like a goodwill dog-and-pony show. I'll never forget how impressed I was by the machinery, all the noise, and the overpowering aromas created by the frying process. Everyone wore white company uniforms and looked neat and clean with their hairnets and caps.

I recently found a cache of old letters written by my parents, including love letters they wrote to each other during the times when they were separated due to work. You can see from Dad's letters to Mom that he was devoted to her. I have learned quite a lot about how the company was grown and about the social part of the business through these letters. One of Dad's letters was written during a trip he made with his brother Earl and his general production superintendent, Roy Boyd, to visit Herman

Our governess Verna Johnson with Willadean (right) and me

The factory floor in Los Angeles

Lay in Atlanta. Lay was one of the first people to have a Frito franchise, and Dad may have made a trip there to check Mr. Lay's operations. After Dad died, there was a merger between Frito and Lay.

Many of Mom's and Dad's letters to each other were written while Dad was opening a new warehouse in San Diego during World War II. During the war, tins of chips were sent overseas to be served in mess halls and sold in PXs. This venture helped put the company over the top as a nationwide business. The San Diego warehouse was opened to service these army contracts. Dad's letters during this time were written on stationery boasting on the letterhead "The Frito Company of California." Mom was a dutiful wife and wrote to Dad almost every day. She wrote rough drafts of her letters on the backs of Frito Company scrap paper and copied the letters over onto pretty stationery with "Mr. and Mrs. C. E. Doolin" printed at the top.

I photocopied all the letters and organized them to give to the rest of the family. At a Sunday family lunch, I gave a copy of the packet to my oldest brother Charles. I decided to

A kettle of steaming corn being emptied into a cooking vat at the California Frito plant

tell everyone about some of the new things I had learned from the letters. First I teased Charles that Dad had nicknamed him "Chongo" in one of his letters. Charles laughed and everyone else joined in. Since Charles was only two at the time the letter was written, he had no memory of Dad calling him by this nickname. Next, I teased Mom that Dad had written "Say hello to the twins" at the end of one of his letters. I couldn't resist saying that I thought this referred either to my brothers Charles and Earl, who seemed like duplicates even though they weren't twins, or else to Mom's breasts. This got a big a laugh from everyone. Someone said, "Surely not!" to my suggestion, and Mom, in her typical way of throwing out little zingers when we least expected them, replied, "If you think not, then you didn't know him very well."

There was one other mystery reference in the letters, to "Tincy," by which I think Dad might have meant "Teensy." (Dad was not a good speller. He even misspelled my name on my birth certificate; it was supposed to be "Kalita," but Dad wrote "Kaleta." As an adult, I considered changing my name to the other spelling but decided to keep Dad's original one for sentimental reasons. My sister's name, Willadean, is another example of Dad's spelling problems; Willadean was named after Dr. Herbert M. Shelton's daughter, Willodeen, as a tribute to a man he very much admired, but obviously Dad didn't quite get the name right.) When I mentioned that the name "Tincy" appeared in one of Dad's letters, Charles suggested it might have referred to me in utero, getting me back for "Chongo." We enjoyed a great brunch, and the packet of letters gave us an entrée into many reflections and questions about the past. ■

Charles and Earl posing for the Bandwagon cover

Recipes

Here's the best meat loaf you ever tasted, and that's not just a Texas brag. I use this meat loaf recipe to this day.

Fritos Texas Loaf (vintage)

❖ Mix the beef, egg, onions, seasonings, and corn chips together. Form into a loaf and place in an oiled pan. Pour the tomatoes over the loaf and bake at 300 degrees for 1 hour.

1	pound ground beef
1	egg
1	large onion, minced
1	clove garlic, minced
½	teaspoon salt
⅛	teaspoon pepper
⅛	teaspoon chili powder
1½	cups crushed Fritos
1	cup canned tomatoes

This recipe promoted Mexene chili powder, which was a new acquisition at the time the recipe was created. Mexene might have been acquired because of the vast quantities of chili powder needed for the Champion Foods Division. I love cumin, and if I had written this vintage recipe I would have made cumin mandatory.

Beef Ole! (vintage)

❖ Brown the beef. Add chili powder and dissolved cumin. Add the spaghetti sauce mix, tomato sauce, and cup of water, combine well, and simmer uncovered for 30 minutes, until the sauce thickens. Serve over a bed of corn chips on a dinner plate. Garnish the top with a spoonful each of shredded lettuce, chopped tomatoes, diced avocado, chopped onions, grated cheese, sliced ripe olives, and whole stuffed olives. Serves 6.

1	pound ground chuck
½	teaspoon Mexene chili powder
½	teaspoon cumin dissolved in 2 teaspoons water (optional)
1	package Lawry's spaghetti sauce mix
1	can (8 ounces) tomato sauce
1	cup water
4	cups Fritos corn chips (regular)
	For garnish: a spoonful each (or to taste) shredded lettuce, chopped tomato, diced avocado, chopped onions, grated cheese, sliced ripe olives, whole stuffed olives

I included the next recipe just for fun. It's a good indicator of the era.

1 pound calf liver (cooked in salted, boiling water and ground)
1 cup broth from cooking liver
1 tablespoon flour
¼ cup chopped onion
¼ cup chopped celery
½ teaspoon salt
¼ teaspoon pepper
½ teaspoon monosodium glutamate (optional)
½ cup crushed Fritos corn chips
2 hard-boiled eggs, chopped
3 slices bacon

Fritos Liver Loaf (vintage)

❖ Cook the liver in boiling, salted water until tender. Put it through a grinder. Thicken the broth with flour. Mix together the liver, broth, onion, celery, seasonings, corn chips, and eggs. Pour into a greased loaf pan. Place bacon slices on top. Bake at 350 degrees for 40 minutes.

Remembering how I learned to spread peanut butter, mayonnaise, and pimento cheese on sandwiches at the Rio Vista Farm when I was a kid reminded me of some recipes that were Miss Ferne's specialties.

3 tablespoons bacon fat (or, update by using oil; use 6 tablespoons if making with venison)
2 pounds ground meat
2 teaspoons ground cumin
3 tablespoons Chili-Quik
1 teaspoon chili powder
½ teaspoon salt
¼ teaspoon pepper
4 large or 5 small garlic cloves, peeled, ground to a pulp in a mortar, and mixed with ¼ cup water
2 cans (7½ ounces each) tomato sauce (Mountain Pass brand preferred), combined with 1 can water
1 can (8 ounces) stewed tomatoes, drained

Miss Ferne's Chili (vintage)

❖ Heat the bacon fat on high. Brown the meat slightly, reduce the heat, and add the rest of the ingredients. Cover and stir often. Bring the mixture to a rolling boil and then turn down the heat to medium-high. Simmer for 45 minutes longer.

2 packages (8 ounces) longhorn-style Natural Cheddar Cheese, grated (sharp preferred but mild is alright)
2½ medium onions, diced very fine
½ cup liquid shortening (Mazola brand is preferred)
2 tablespoons Masa Harina
1 tablespoon Chili-Quik
1 cup water
22 tortillas
1 +1 cups Miss Ferne's Chili

Miss Ferne's Rio Vista Enchiladas (vintage)

❖ Preheat the oven to 350 degrees. Heat a skillet on medium. Assemble the cheese (reserving some to put on the top) and the onions. Heat the shortening, add the Masa Harina and Chili-Quik, and brown. Add the cup of water and stir. Dip the tortillas in this sauce one at a time, sprinkle them down the center with the onion-and-cheese mixture, roll them up, and place them in a large pan. Cover with 1 cup of the chili. Add 1 cup of water to the other cup of chili chili to make a thin sauce and pour over the enchiladas. Put in the oven, heat thoroughly, remove, and sprinkle with the remaining cheese. Cover to melt and keep warm.

My brother Charles remembers Miss Ferne's meat spread as something special. Alma Colston, Miss Ferne's second daughter, described the meat spread this way: "Mom would grind whatever meat she had left over, would add chopped pickles, grated cheese, sometimes grated onion, diced tomatoes, and chopped lettuce, and would mix mayo with it. You could either eat it like a sandwich, on crackers, or just by itself. I liked to eat it with Fritos, kind of like a dip."

Below you'll also find several recipes I found in the big Nell Morris scrapbook for spreads that could be eaten on sandwiches or crackers such as Melba toast.

Fritos Peanut Butter Spread (vintage)

❖ Mix together peanut butter, mayonnaise, and Fritos corn chips. Spread on bread to form sandwiches. Serve more Fritos on the plate beside the sandwiches.

½ cup crunchy peanut butter
2 tablespoons mayonnaise
½ cup Fritos corn chips, finely crushed
6 slices bread

The next recipe was touted as "very tasty with your favorite beverage and ideal for the children's lunches."

Fritos Pimento-Cheese Spread (vintage)

❖ Mix the corn chips with the pimento-cheese spread. Spread on bread.

½ cup Fritos corn chips, finely crushed
1 jar (5 ounces) pimento-cheese spread
12 slices rye or white bread

Fritos Olive Butter and Cheese Spread (vintage)

❖ Moisten the cream cheese with the milk. Add the olive butter and mix. Add the crushed corn chips and use as a spread.

1 package (3 ounces) cream cheese
4 tablespoons milk
2 tablespoons olive butter
¼ cup Fritos corn chips, crushed

Chapter 4

Diversification

D AD DECIDED to diversify into potato chips and various other snack foods long before he met Herman Lay. I found a letter Dad wrote to his parents (he addresses them as "Papa and Mama") in 1934, soon after his move to Dallas to open a new headquarters. In the letter he writes, "I experimented with potato chips last night and although not entirely successful, [the result] was satisfactory. Expect to straighten it out today. Will soon be in the potato chip business here in Dallas, which will stabilize our business. The Frito business as a business is recognized as a 'risk' by the bank . . . while the potato chip business is considered a 'stable' business. By this fall, I plan to be making good potato chips, good peanuts, and good Fritos."

Eventually, of course, the company diversified into a variety of new snack foods, including Fritatos, Efsees, Fluffs, Cheetos, Ruffles, Doritos, Munchos, Funyuns, Frenchips, Rold Gold Pretzels, Tostitos, Stax, and more. Fritatos were the result of the potato-chip-cooking experiments Dad refers in the letter above. Fritatos were introduced to the public in 1935. Eventually their name was shortened to "Tatos" and now, of course, they're called "Lay's® Potato Chips." Efsees, introduced in 1937, were peanut butter cracker sandwiches. Their name pronounces the initials of the Frito Company. (Dad's marketing prowess seems to have failed him on this one.) In addition to Efsees the company produced and distributed bags of salted peanuts and had done so since its early days. Fluffs were fried pork skins, or "cracklin's," as they're called in the South. Fluffs were introduced in 1941. According to my half-brother Ronald, when Fluffs were first produced the pork skins were stretched and stapled to boards and cut by hand. In 1954 my Uncle Earl invented and patented a tool with a long row of blades that could be drawn across the stretched pork skin to make the strips. Fluffs are now called

Photo of an original glassine bag for Fritatos, the first generation of Frito Company potato chips

FOOD
PRODUCTS
OF
The Frito Company

"Baken-ets." Cheetos were introduced in 1950; in the little kitchen next to his office Dad developed the powdered cheese flavoring that coated Cheetos.

The process for the puffed corn used in Cheetos was licensed from the Adams Company. Dad named the new product *Cheetos*

because he believed that names ending in "o" were highly marketable. He believed, and eventually proved, that using o's at the ends of all his products' names would give them name-brand recognition. These days this practice is called "branding." When I make my own homemade corn chips I call them "Kaletos," as a nod to Dad. Mom told me that the original name ending in "o," Frito, is derived from *frit,* which is Spanish for "fried," and *ito,* which means "little." So the name Fritos is Spanish for "little fries."

In the late 1950s Dad was experimenting with products made with dehydrated potatoes, but he told my mother that the public wasn't ready for them yet. Eventually, after Dad's death, dehydrated potato chips came into their own and the company introduced Munchos.

I remember when Munchos were test-marketed by the Frito Company. It was during the year I graduated from high school; I served my friends their first taste of Munchos during my graduation party. Munchos are still manufactured, but Stax have joined them in the Frito-Lay potato crisps category. Stax, which are curved spoon-like and stacked together in oval tubes, are competing successfully with Pringles in the marketplace. They're similar to Munchos; the company changed the shape, formula, name, and packaging, and changed the place of manufacture to a plant in Mexico.

Although Doritos were produced long after Dad's death, he was always interested in developing and producing tortilla chips; in fact, his original idea, before he even started the Frito Company, was to go into business with Tony's Toasted Tortillas, a Texas-based company that existed at the time. (See appendix 3, "Letter from C. E. Doolin to the *Frito Bandwagon,*" for the whole story of this, told in my father's own words.) It's interesting to me that Dad was always so on-target in predicting the tastes of the future.

I recently learned that Fritos acquired Doritos (which were probably called something else in their original form), and the process for making them, from Alex Foods in California. Doritos as a brand name made its debut in 1965. Nell Morris developed a ton of recipes using Doritos. Some of them are included at the end of this chapter.

In 1952 the Frito Company purchased a canning business called Champion Chili. In 1956 it purchased another canning company, Texas Tavern, and then merged the two into one division called Champion Foods. The new division could be seen as part of the Cooking with Fritos marketing strategy, since Fritos Chili Pie, a recipe that was widely distributed in grocery stores as part of the company's marketing campaign, combines Fritos with chili. Champion Foods produced a variety of canned foods and dried mixes. The list of Champion Food products was extensive and almost completely Mexican-inspired.

Champion Foods also made the fare served at Casa de Fritos in Disneyland. Dad was in on the ground floor of Disneyland. He opened a restaurant there using Ta-Cups (see chapter 6, "Inventors and Inventions," for a description of these), chips, and

YOU GET 25¢

...for discovering the better quality of

FRITOS BRAND CHILI

Taste for yourself! It's the *only* way to discover the better quality of Fritos Brand Chili. You'll find more good lean beef...more flavor that comes from selected spices used with knowing care. This is the chili you've always wished someone would make. Chili with real homemade flavor — Fritos Brand Chili!

You'll get 25¢ back if you mail us the label from Fritos Brand Chili before Feb. 29, 1960.

Limit: Four refunds to a family.

USE THIS HANDY COUPON

The Frito Company
Dept. B
P. O. Box 5235
Dallas 22, Texas
Enclosed is the label from Fritos Brand Chili, for which I will receive a refund of 25¢ by return mail.
Name
Address
City_____ Zone_____ State_____
Where purchased
Offer expires Feb. 29, 1960. Limit: 4 refunds per family.

In 1952 the Frito Company purchased a canning business called Champion Chili. This 1960 money-back incentive promotion was just one the winning Fritos Pie marketing concepts.

Ingredients for Fritos Chili Pie, captured by a food photographer. This photo was sent to food editors at magazines and newspapers.

canned foods from the Champion Foods Division. He experimented with early fast food in this venue. I have read that he was very excited by his location in Disneyland, across from the exit to the Jungle Ride in Frontierland. The restaurant was later moved to a spot adjacent to the Mine Ride so its square footage could be expanded. The restaurant had a wonderful mechanized talking Frito Kid figure with a dispenser for five-cent bags of Fritos. The bags came down a mining chute to land within reach at the bottom. The mechanized figure was programmed with different recordings in rotation. I thought that it was Disney's magic at work and in fact it may have been developed by the Disney workshop. The women behind the counters in the restaurant sported colorful, ruffled, Mexican-looking uniforms with ruffled-ribbon hair combs worn like little tiaras. ■

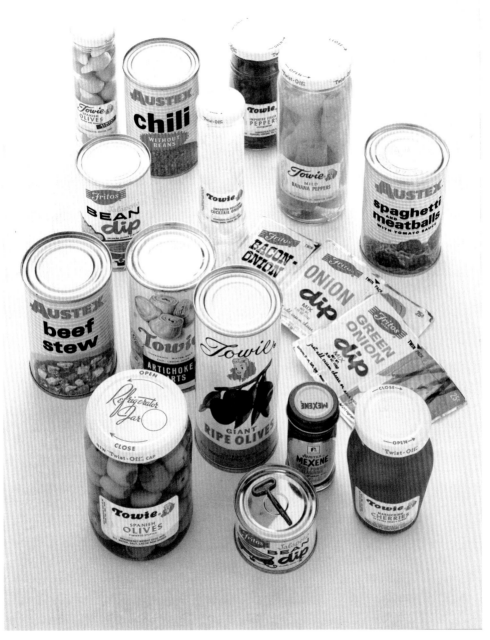

New acquisitions of Belle Products, including Towie cherries and olives, Mexene Chili Powder, and Austex brand products. From the PepsiCo, Inc. Annual Report, *1966.*

Casa de Fritos, Dad's experimental restaurant at Disneyland.

Mary Livingston with W. H. Foster, treasurer of the Western Division of the Frito Company, in front of the Riverboat ride at Disneyland.

Recipes

Here are some vintage recipes using potato chips and pretzels.

Green Bean Casserole with Potato Chips (vintage)

❖ Drain the green beans and add to the condensed celery soup. Pour into a greased casserole. Sprinkle the top with the crushed potato chips and grated cheese. Bake at 350 degrees for 30 minutes or until bubbly. Serves 6–8.

2 cups cooked green beans (or canned), drained
1 can (10½ ounces) condensed cream of celery soup
½ cup crushed potato chips
4 tablespoons grated American cheese

Squash and Onion Casserole (vintage)

❖ Pare the squashes, peel the onion, and cut them all into medium slices. Boil in the salted water or steam until tender. Drain the water off and add the seasonings and bacon drippings. Pour into a greased casserole. Top with the grated cheese and crushed potato chips. Bake at 350 degrees for 20 minutes. Serves 6.

6 medium summer squashes (yellow or white)
1 medium onion
1½ cups boiling, salted water
1½ teaspoons salt
¼ teaspoon pepper
3 tablespoons bacon drippings
½ cup grated American cheese
½ cup lightly crushed potato chips

Chick'n Pretzel Pie (vintage)

❖ Line a lightly greased 2-quart casserole or baking dish with 1 cup of the crushed pretzels. In a large mixing bowl, blend the remaining crushed pretzels with the chicken, eggs, green pepper, onion, mushrooms, and pimento. Put the mixture into the casserole. Blend the remaining ingredients (other than for garnish) in a saucepan and simmer, covered, for 5 minutes. Stir and pour evenly over the casserole. Bake at 350 degrees for about 25 minutes. Garnish with the strips of breast meat, sliced egg, and whole pretzels. Serves 6–8.

1 + 2 cups coarsely crushed pretzels + whole pretzels for garnish
2 cups cooked chicken, cut into pieces, + strips of breast meat for garnish
3 hard-cooked eggs, chopped, + 1 sliced for garnish
1 medium green pepper, chopped
½ cup chopped onion
1 can (3 ounces) sliced mushrooms, undrained
1 can (4 ounces) pimento, undrained and chopped
1 can (10½ ounces) condensed cream of chicken soup
½ cup milk or chicken stock
1 teaspoon Worcestershire sauce
½ teaspoon paprika
⅛ teaspoon ground pepper
1 clove garlic, crushed (optional)
Extra sliced egg, strips of breast meat, and whole pretzels for garnish

1 cup evaporated milk
1 egg
1½ pounds ground beef
1 cup pretzel crumbs
1 medium onion, finely chopped
1 can (4 ounces) mushrooms
¾ teaspoon salt
¼ cup monosodium glutamate (optional)
⅛ teaspoon thyme (optional)
⅛ teaspoon savory (optional)
⅛ teaspoon marjoram (optional)

Pretzel Meat Loaf (vintage)

❖ Beat the evaporated milk and egg in a mixing bowl. Add the ground beef and mix well. Add the pretzel crumbs and remaining ingredients, again mixing well. Form into a loaf and place in a greased, shallow baking pan. Bake at 350 degrees for 1 hour. Serves 6.

2 cans (11½ ounces) condensed Campbell's Manhandler's Bean with Bacon Soup
½ cup water
A large handful of whole Doritos
½ cup finely chopped onion
½ cup grated Cheddar cheese
½ cup crushed Doritos Nacho Cheese Flavored Tortilla Chips

Hearty Bean Casserole (vintage)

❖ Blend the soup and water and heat. Place the tortilla chips in a 1½-quart casserole. Sprinkle the onion over the chips and then pour the soup over. Top with the grated cheese and the crushed tortilla chips. Bake at 350 degrees for 20 minutes. Serves 6.

1 pound ground beef
¼ cup chopped onion
2 cups tomato sauce
1 teaspoon salt
A large handful of Doritos Nacho Cheese Flavored Tortilla Chips, ⅓ of them crushed
1 + 1 cups grated Cheddar cheese

Beef Casserole (vintage)

❖ Sauté the beef in a skillet until light in color and then add the onion and cook until tender. Add the tomato sauce and salt. Place the ⅔ handful of whole tortilla chips in a 1½-quart greased casserole. Sprinkle 1 cup of the grated cheese over the chips. Add the beef and onion mixture. Crush the remaining ⅓ handful of crushed tortilla chips. Top with the remaining cheese and the crushed chips. Bake at 350 degrees for 15 minutes. Serves 6.

A large handful of Doritos Nacho Cheese Flavored Tortilla Chips, divided into ⅔ and ⅓
2 cups canned tomatoes
¾ teaspoon salt
¼ teaspoon pepper
1 cup grated cheese

Aztec Casserole (vintage)

❖ Place the ⅔ handful of tortilla chips in a 1½-quart greased casserole. Combine the tomatoes and seasonings and pour over the chips. Garnish with the grated cheese and remaining ⅓ handful of tortilla chips by standing the chips around the edge of the casserole. Bake at 350 degrees for 20 minutes. Serves 6.

The following recipes for Tex-Mex food, published in booklets distributed by the Cooking with Fritos campaign in the 1940s and 1950s, used canned foods made by Champion Foods. They were probably also the recipes for dishes served at Casa de Fritos at Disneyland.

Fritos Tamale Loaf (vintage)

❖ Combine the first 5 ingredients. Lightly sauté the garlic and meat in the fat, then add the chili powder and tomatoes. Simmer 5 minutes and combine with the creamed-corn mixture. Add the beaten eggs and olives and mix together. Bake in a greased loaf pan at 350 degrees for 1 hour. Serves 6 generously and is good warmed over.

1 can (17 ounces) cream-style corn
1 bag (4 ounces) Fritos corn chips
2 teaspoons salt
¼ teaspoon pepper
¼ teaspoon dried basil (optional)
1 clove garlic, minced
½ pound ground beef *or* 1 tightly packed cup ground, cooked, leftover meat
2 tablespoons fat
1 teaspoon chili powder
1¼ cups canned tomatoes
2 eggs, beaten
24 ripe olives

Tamale Royal (also called "Fritos Tamale-Adas") (vintage)

❖ Place a layer of tamales in a casserole. Add the tamale gravy, cover with half the onions and cheese, and repeat, adding the corn chips last. Heat in the oven until thoroughly hot and the cheese is melted. Serves 6.

12 tamales
4 tablespoons canned tamale gravy
¼ + ¼ cup chopped onion
½ + ½ cup grated cheese
½ cup crushed Fritos corn chips

Fritos Enchiladas (vintage)

❖ Place half of the crushed Fritos in buttered casserole; pour half the can of chili or enchilada sauce over the Fritos. Top this with half of the chopped onion and ½ cup of the grated cheese. Repeat the layers again and bake in a 350-degree oven for 20 minutes, or long enough to warm and melt the cheese without cooking the onions thoroughly.

1 bag (4 ounces) Fritos corn chips, crushed
1 large can chili without beans *or*
1 can enchilada sauce
2 large onions, chopped
1 cup grated American cheese

Chapter 5
Cattle and Corn

E VEN THOUGH my father is best known as the premier founder of the Frito Company, he had his finger in many pies, and he was an active, creative, and wide-ranging entrepreneur. Hybridizing corn; cross-breeding cattle (Brahma bulls with Black Angus cows, producing a hardier cross-breed of Brangus cattle for sale), developing, selling, and finding new uses for cold-rolled sesame oil; and developing experimental hog and cattle feeds from byproducts of his other ventures—these were Dad's interests along with the snack and fast food businesses. Interesting that Dad was in the cattle business, since he and our family followed a vegetarian diet. My mom told me that the cattle operation kept the Frito Company afloat in some of the early years.

There were Frito Farms all over Texas. My father personally owned all of them (at least at the time of his death; at one point

Here is one of the Brahma bulls Dad used to produce a herd of crossbred Brangus cattle. These were more drought-hardy cattle for the Texas climate.

he and my Uncle Earl co-owned the Rio Vista Farm) and used them to develop products for his businesses and to raise cattle and hogs. According to the *Frito Bandwagon,* "the motivating factor for establishing the farms was cultivation of the soil, for from soil grows good corn."

The Rio Vista, so named because the Nueces River ran

◀ *Dad with a shed full of grain at the Rio Vista Farm in January 1955*

▼ *Dad driving a newly acquired "Bush Hog" at the Rio Vista farm*

through it, was the first of the Frito Farms. It was a 1,200-acre experimental farm where cattle were raised and corn and sesame plants were grown. The Doolin family owned the Rio Vista in the early 1940s and probably earlier, and as I have mentioned, my grandfather and his second wife, Miss Ferne, worked there as foreman and bookkeeper.

Another Frito Farm was in Poteet. When we went to the Rio Vista to see my grandfather Coleman and his family, we would stop at the farm in Poteet on the way. Peanuts grown for their oil were the main crop there; at that time peanut oil was included in the vegetable oil mix used to fry Fritos. The peanuts grown at Poteet were also used in the company's Efsees peanut butter cracker sandwiches and in bags of salted peanuts.

After July 1953, the Frito Company had a subsidiary in San Antonio called the Texas Vegetable Oil Company, which manufactured cooking oils such as corn, peanut, and sesame oils, from the nuts and seeds of plants Dad grew on his farms. (When I arrived in 1962 at a boarding school in Switzerland in a huge Cadillac limo with a driver, which Mom had arranged to take my sister and two of my brothers and me to our various schools in Europe, my fellow students made the assumption that, being from Texas, I was an oil heiress—little did they know the oil was *cooking* oil.)

Our governess Verna Johnson with my youngest brother Danny on the banks of the Nueces River at the Rio Vista farm. My sister and I are in the background.

The Texas Tavern Canning Company, which was part of the Champion Foods Division, was located in Seguin. We often stopped in Seguin to visit the canning company before stopping at the farm in Poteet—Poteet and Seguin were both in the San Antonio vicinity. It was an eight-hour drive from Dallas to the Rio Vista ranch, when you drove straight through. My siblings and I fought most of the way, and when we stopped at the canning company in Seguin we groaned with boredom, although it was a relief to get out of the car and breathe some fresh air.

When the farm in Poteet had some peanut crop overages, John Middleton, vice president of the Texas Vegetable Oil Company, bought young dairy cattle to fatten on the leftovers. Eventually the cattle took over and replaced the peanuts and other crops—guar beans and soybeans were also grown experimentally at Poteet in the early years—and the experimental farm in Poteet became a small feedlot. (These days, the town of Poteet, which is in the middle of the Texas hill country, holds an annual strawberry festival, and regional chefs buy fresh produce there

Here are cattle feeding on Dad's experimental pellets. One of his recipes incorporated mesquite.

on a regular basis. "Hill country" is a vernacular term applied to a region including all or part of twenty-five counties near the geographical center of Texas. Recipes made from regional foods grown in the Texas hill country are considered by some chefs to be comparable to the cuisine of Provence.)

Another Frito Farm was near the town of Midlothian. Midlothian, as we always called the farm, was purchased after the Rio Vista and Poteet and was only an hour's drive from our house. It was mostly used for farming experiments. At the same time that the company bought Midlothian, it also acquired another experimental farm in east Texas near Henderson.

The Rio Vista grew different hybrids of corn for the Frito Company to test. Helen Harden, a long-time employee of the Frito Company, told me that Dad developed his own strain of corn on the farm: "He hired a young man who had a degree in agronomy and he literally formed a hybrid of sweet corn and field corn." He did this because "some people like field corn, which has a strong husk on it, and some people do not like it. And so he developed his own corn. . . . He had a little kitchen [next to his office] and he'd go into his kitchen and put things together, and sometimes he'd say to me, 'Helen I want you to

Renner soybeans were one of the experimental crops grown on the Frito farms.

taste this and see [how you like it].'" Helen told me that Dad developed many flavorings for chips and other products in that kitchen.

Dad's involvement in the farming and ranching part of the business was obsessively thorough, as was his involvement in every aspect of the company. His capacity for juggling so many things at once, and in such detail, is mind-boggling. At the farm in Poteet, Dad ordered the fields to be planted with Blue Buffle and Harding grasses, which are hardy enough to survive drought and weather extremes including winter cold. After my grandfather Coleman lost eight head of Rio Vista cattle, valued at $880 total, to diseases that might have been prevented by using a different vaccine, Dad advised my grandfather that in the future the cattle should be vaccinated with something called "four-way vaccine." He also told my grandfather to have the cattle vaccinated on purchase at the stockyard because it was done by a federal employee and therefore didn't cost anything for the labor. Dad also raised oat hay at the Rio Vista for the cattle on all of the Frito Farms. He advised that it be cured green— that is, baled while the leaves and stalks were still green, and he ordered that the calves be fed on an oat hay and cottonseed

Cattle pens at the Rio Vista Frito farm

meal. Each was to have ten to fourteen pounds of oat hay daily, plus three-quarters to one pound of cottonseed meal and some molasses syrup.

Dad must have been involved up to his eyebrows with so many details. No wonder every Sunday we were going to his farm in Midlothian. He was doing business on the day of rest, conducting research pertaining to hog feed (Fritos Hog Chow X) and sesame crops. There were also dairy cows at Midlothian. Dad was fattening the Guernsey calves to sell, and while my brothers and sister and I were catching crawdads in a flooded area at the end of the road, he would be checking on the progress of his calves.

Sesame seeds come from the seedpod heads of tall plants with huge tobacco-like leaves. At the Midlothian farm Dad planted what was then a new strain of sesame plants. It had been developed by Dr. Derald G. Langham, and it produced sesame-seed heads that didn't pop open and could therefore be harvested. The Southwest Agricultural Institute collaborated with Dad in this endeavor, with various agronomists going to the farm to measure and document the progress of the plants and test the effect of the sometimes-severe Texas climate on the crop. Dad

Hampshire hogs fed on Dad's experimental hog feed at the Midlothian farm. Dad had so many enterprises going concurrently. Every Sunday we were going to this nearby farm.

received national recognition for his contribution to determining the strain of sesame most suitable for growing in Texas. His small experimental crop at Midlothian helped lay the groundwork for today's U.S. production of sesame; as of April 2000, fifty thousand acres were planted with it, mostly in Texas.

In addition to planting sesame crops, Dad was experimenting with extracting and processing cold-rolled sesame oil, which is more stable than other oils—it doesn't get rancid as fast. The company first tested sesame oil imported from Asia in 1936.

After the Frito Company acquired the Texas Vegetable Oil Company, Texas Vegetable Oil put most of its emphasis on sesame oil production and by early 1958 began marketing filtered sesame oil "for the health food trade," according to the *Frito Bandwagon.*

Dad also began experimenting with developing products that used sesame seeds, including two different kinds of sesame candy. Sesame pralines were one; the other, Sesame Crunch, was included in the menu featuring Fritos recipes served at a food convention in Ohio. ■

▼ *Kaleta and John Campbell posing with sesame seeds for Mom's Viewmaster camera.*

◄ *At the Midlothian farm Dad planted what was then a new strain of sesame plants. It had been developed by Dr. Derald G. Langham, and it produced sesame-seed heads that didn't pop open and could therefore be harvested.*

*Dad (right) with John Campbell
inspecting sesame ricks at harvest
time*

Recipes

Here I present a group of corn and corn-derived recipes in honor of my father's development of his own corn hybrid, the yellow and white variety. I have also included a recipe for Spoon Bread (my spontaneous-dinner-party find).

Fritos Crackling Bread (vintage)

❖ Sift the dry ingredients together, add the egg beaten with milk, and stir well. Add the melted shortening and then stir in broken corn chips. Bake at 350 degrees for 1 hour, and serve hot.

1 cup white cornmeal
2 teaspoons baking powder
¼ teaspoon salt
1 egg, beaten with a little milk
1 teaspoon shortening, melted
½ cup Fritos corn chips, broken

Kaleta's Pantry Spoon Bread

❖ Scald the milk and add the cornmeal, stirring constantly. Add the butter, sugar, cayenne, and salt. Slightly beat the egg yolks and add them. Then beat the egg whites and baking powder until stiff and fold them in. Bake in a greased casserole at 350 degrees for 45 minutes, until firm.

3 cups milk
1 cup white cornmeal
2 tablespoons butter, melted
1 teaspoon sugar
¾ teaspoon cayenne
1 teaspoon salt
3 egg whites, beaten until stiff
1 teaspoon baking powder

Today, steam-in-the-package vegetables, including corn, make the canned corn used in the following recipe obsolete. Steamed corn is much more nutritious than canned corn—I recommend substituting it in this recipe.

Corn Pudding

❖ Combine the corn, flour, butter, sugar, and salt. In a separate bowl combine the eggs, milk, and cream. Combine the mixtures, pour into a greased baking dish, and bake at 350 degrees for 1 hour. Stir several times during the first half hour.

2 cups canned corn, drained
4 tablespoons flour
1 tablespoon butter, melted
2 teaspoons sugar
1 teaspoon salt
2 eggs, well beaten
1 cup milk
1 cup cream
Fritos corn chips

I've included some vintage dip recipes below. All of them end with instructions to serve them with Fritos corn chips.

When king-size chips were invented for dips in 1947, recipes by Daisy Dean appeared on the backs of the larger bags. The majority of these recipes were for dips. Many of them used ▶

▶▶ products made by the company's canning division. They can be changed according to your taste—for example, goat cheese can be substituted for cream cheese or sour cream. When I was a kid my mother made up her own dip recipes using a blend of sour cream, cream cheese, and Frito Company packaged, dehydrated flavoring mixes.

The next recipe calls for onion juice, which could be bought in the 1950s and 1960s in a brown glass onion-shaped container. You can make your own onion juice by putting chopped onion into a food processor or blender and blending it until it's liquefied, then putting it through a strainer.

---

2 packages cream cheese
3 ounces (or to taste) Roquefort cheese
1 tablespoon heavy cream
¼ teaspoon onion juice
1 tablespoon sherry wine
   Fritos corn chips

Roquefort Dip (vintage)

❖ Blend all the ingredients. Mix well. Let stand a few hours. Serve with corn chips.

---

2 packages (3 ounces each) cream cheese
6 tablespoons milk
5 ounces blue cheese
⅛ teaspoon garlic salt
¼ teaspoon hot sauce
½ cup chopped, toasted pecans
   King-size Fritos corn chips

Fritos Blue Cheese Dip (vintage)

❖ Soften the cream cheese with the milk and then blend with the blue cheese. Add the remaining ingredients, mix together, and serve as a dip with the corn chips.

---

2 (3 ounces each) packages cream cheese
¼ cup crumbled Roquefort cheese
¼ cup whole milk
2 teaspoons lemon juice
1 teaspoon Worcestershire sauce
2 tablespoons mayonnaise
2 teaspoons minced parsley + more parsley for garnish
2 teaspoons minced onion
1 bag (8 ounces) Fritos corn chips

Fritos Cheese Dip (also called "Fritos Philly Dip") (vintage)

❖ Allow the cream cheese to reach room temperature and add the Roquefort cheese. Slowly add the milk, beating thoroughly. (Use a mixer if possible.) Add the remaining ingredients except for the corn chips and continue beating until the mixture is of a consistency suitable for dunking without dripping. Pour into a serving bowl and garnish with paprika and more parsley if desired. Dunk the corn chips in the mixture. Serves about 8.

VARIATIONS

❖ Roquefort cheese may be omitted and 1 teaspoon of anchovy paste (or three whole, finely chopped anchovies) may be substituted. The serving bowl may be rubbed with a cut garlic clove and, if a stronger dip is desired, 1 medium garlic clove mashed to a fine paste may be used in place of onion.

This recipe has always been one of my favorites, but I prefer to eat it with potato chips rather than corn chips.

Fritos Clam-Cheese Dip (vintage)

❖ Mix the cream cheese with the lemon juice, salt, Worcestershire sauce, clam liquid, and garlic. Add the clams, mix together, and serve as a dip with the Fritos.

3 packages (3 ounces each) cream cheese
1 teaspoon lemon juice
1 teaspoon salt
1 teaspoon Worcestershire sauce
2 tablespoons clam liquid
1 clove garlic, finely cut (optional)
1 can (7½ ounces) minced clams, drained
3 cups Fritos corn chips

I prefer not to use packaged processed cheese food in the following dishes, although that's a fast and easy way to make them and was recommended in the original recipes. My mother used Wisconsin Cheddar cheese in her own cheese sauce recipes, and I've substituted that in these recipes.

Fritos Con Queso (vintage)

❖ Put a layer of corn chips in a casserole dish. Cover with the onions. Add the grated cheese and place in a 350-degree oven until the cheese melts. Serve with more corn chips.

1 cup Fritos corn chips + more to serve
½ cup onions, chopped
4 ounces Wisconsin Cheddar cheese, grated

Fritos Hot Cheese Dip (vintage)

❖ Combine the tomatoes and cubed cheese. Heat over a low flame until the cheese is melted, stirring continuously. Serve hot with the corn chips.

½ can (10 ounces) tomatoes and green chilies
4 ounces Wisconsin cheese, cubed
Fritos corn chips

Ja-tos Basic Dip (vintage)

❖ Soften the cheese and cream until smooth. Add the remaining ingredients and mix together. Serve with the corn chips.

VARIATIONS
❖ Add 2 cloves crushed garlic or 2 teaspoons anchovy paste.

1 package (8 ounces) cream cheese
1 teaspoon salt
Dash cayenne pepper
1 teaspoon lemon juice
4 tablespoons cream
2 tablespoons mayonnaise
2 teaspoons onion juice
Fritos corn chips

Corn and beans are a Mexican tradition. In Mexico corn tortillas rolled up with beans inside have been eaten for centuries. With the help of my father and others, this combination has become popular in America in the form of vegetarian tacos and other Mexican-American dishes.

The Fritos Bean Dip recipes below were developed by Nell Morris. All are to be served with Fritos.

Fritos Bean Dip Variations

❖ Blend 2 parts Fritos Bean Dip with 1 part of any of these:

- Cream cheese,
- Deviled ham, *or*
- Pasteurized processed cheese spread

OR, TRY COMBINING

- 2 parts Fritos Bean Dip with 1 part deviled ham *or*
- 3 parts of the bean dip with 1 part liver paté.

You can serve any of these on hamburger patties and all of them with Fritos corn chips.

Fritos Surprise à la Nutella (original)

By Kaleta Doolin

❖ A delicious vegetable-and-nut dessert—chocolaty, sweet, and salty. Just dip your Fritos into Nutella hazelnut chocolate spread. It's a knockout.

I couldn't find the original recipe for Dad's sesame crunch so I reconstructed it, using an old family recipe for peanut brittle and substituting toasted sesame seeds. The peanut brittle recipe was developed by my great-aunt, Bess Dennis, and collected by me. During the 1970s Aunt Bess brought her peanut brittle to a family reunion and I interviewed her about the recipe then. I wrote it all down in Bess's words, some of which I've retained below. (If you'd like to make peanut brittle instead of sesame crunch, use raw peanuts instead of sesame seeds.)

3 cups sugar
1½ cups light corn syrup
¾ cup hot water
4 cups toasted sesame seeds
1 heaping teaspoon soda
1½ teaspoons margarine
1½ teaspoons vanilla

Sesame Crunch (vintage, reconstructed)

By Kaleta Doolin and Bess Dennis

❖ Combine the sugar, corn syrup, and water. Cook until it strings. Add the sesame seeds and cook until the seeds are nutty-smelling and the color of the candy turns golden. Add the soda, margarine, and vanilla. "Set it off the fire. Stir like hell for about 1 min." Pour the mixture onto a greased cookie sheet and let it cool.

Chapter 6

Inventors and Inventions

D AD WAS constantly coming up with ideas to help sales, and he liked to tinker and invent devices that would improve the business. He and my Uncle Earl learned about patents from my paternal grandfather, C. B. Doolin, a steam engineer who owned a garage where he repaired steam engines. He also sold tires—vehicle tires were solid rubber at the time. In 1919, Grandfather Doolin invented and patented laminated tire casings (creating "belted" tires) as well as accessories for Model Ts. According to Mom, glass bud vases in cars were his idea. He also invented and applied for the patent for an apparatus

▼ Dad's patented design for a carhop tray. Dad was in on the ground floor of developments in the fast food industry as well as in the snack food business.

◀ Dad got the idea for his carhop tray from his father. This was my grandfather's prototype. He did not win a patent, but Dad's modified version did.

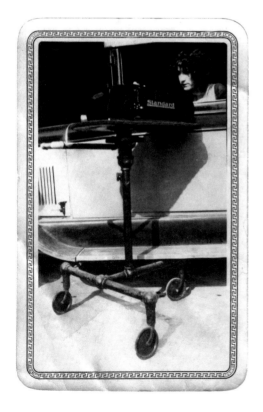

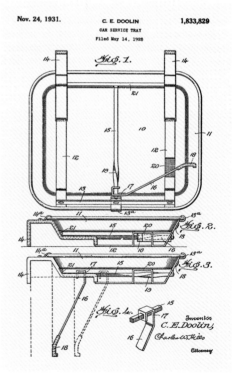

Nov. 24, 1931.   C. E. DOOLIN   1,833,829
CAR SERVICE TRAY
Filed May 14, 1928

for carhops to use when serving food at drive-ins, but it wasn't granted—later my father's modified version of this device did win a patent.

My grandfather also tried to patent an oil can with a flexible metal hose. The patent application was for both the oil can and the metal hose. Neither of these patents was granted. Mother told me that my grandfather was especially upset about not being awarded a patent for the flexible metal hose, since these have so many uses, including as gooseneck lamp bases and refrigerator hoses. (See appendix 4 for a complete list of Doolin family patents.)

The Frito Company's early history abounds with inventions and with patents on newly invented items, such as the clip racks in grocery store aisles that we now take for granted. According to the *Frito Bandwagon,* when my father saw Olguin's "crudely packaged snack food" in a cookie jar on the counter of a gas station café, he saw it as a product that would lend itself to merchandising from display racks—an idea he had envisioned several years previously. It's amazing to think about how important these early patents were to the success of the Frito Company. They were important partly because these items gave the company an edge as well as added income when competitors paid royalties to use them. (For example, Church's Fried Chicken has and continues to use my father's deep-fryer invention.)

One of my father's inventions was the Ta-Cup. This was a kind of taco shell that was shaped like a small round tart. Dad created a tool to make the first Ta-Cup. He sent the tool to the patent office with an application, and they returned this original Ta-Cup-maker when they awarded him the patent. Twenty years ago I found this prototype stored on a shelf in an outbuilding on my mother's property, underneath Dad's old workbench.

My father's bench was stained dark brown and smelled of oil, presumably from engineering projects he did at home. When I was a little girl I sometimes got to have one-on-one time with Dad in his workshop at home. My job was to replace the tools on the pegboard where he had drawn their outlines in white and had written their names. Dad made his own tool hangers for the pegboard; he made them on a bending machine, which was clamped into the jaws of his bench vise. (Uncle Earl had a bending machine too. My brother Charles told me that both machines were made at the same time in the Fritos machine shop.)

My father's original Ta-Cup–making tool consists of two metal tart molds that fit one inside the other and with holes burned in the bottom one. A tortilla pressed between the two cups would be molded into a scalloped cup-shape and fried crisp when the Ta-Cup maker was dipped in hot oil and the oil seeped in through the holes. The apparatus was held together with two

◀ *Grandfather's oil can. This was the prototype for the patent application.*

▼ *Drawings for my grandfather's patent application for an oil can with measuring capability and a flexible hose. This was before the time oil was sold in small, premeasured amounts. This one didn't fly—the patent was denied.*

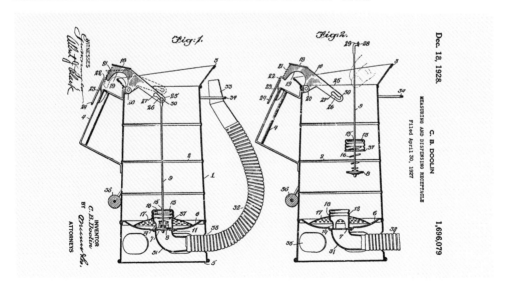

spring steel handles and operated like kitchen tongs. To this day my father's prototype for the Ta-Cup maker sits on my fireplace mantle, next to my grandfather's prototype for the oil can with its flexible metal hose.

When I went through Dad's papers, I found that he was anxious to rush the Ta-Cup to patent. His memos to the Frito Company legal department about the patent were most imperative. Apparently someone else had had the same idea and there was a close race. I wonder if the patent has lapsed and whether the tortilla bowls that are popular now for taco salads pay royalties to Frito-Lay. I understand that you have to police your own inventions to protect them from becoming common usage.

Dad worked with an engineer, Wid Gunderson, to make a machine for mass production of his tortillas molded into cup shapes, and he bought a chain of fifteen Dairy Marts in which he used the new, mass-produced Ta-Cups to make a variety of Mexican fast foods. He also test-marketed the Ta-Cup at several other fast food chains, including Pig Stand in Dallas (which served barbecued pork sandwiches) and Shady Oaks Drive-In in Fort Worth. The Ta-Cup was very popular at the Shady Oaks, selling 176 Ta-Cups in one weekend. The Ta-Cup did less well at Pig Stand, selling only 40 during the same weekend. An advertisement for the Ta-Cup, which I found in Nell Morris's scrapbook, reads as follows: "Ask for 'Tah-cups.' Corn Masa Pastry

▼ *Dad experimenting with the Ta-Cup concept at home*

▶ ▶ *Handmade Ta-Cup prototype. This was later made into a mass production machine. The patent-winning prototype sits on my mantle with other treasured memorabilia.*

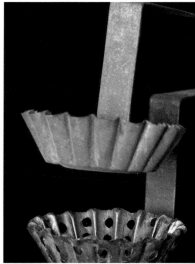

Shells For Preparing Tacos and Other Mexican Dishes in exciting new ways. Made by the makers of Fritos®."

According to Mom Dad's deep-fryer inventions had a control that sensed when the frying food was cooked. She said that everything cooked in the fryer came out a uniform color. Looking at the registered patents, it looks as though Uncle Earl must have held the patent and Dad must have bought it when he bought Uncle Earl's share of the company. My Uncle Earl and my father also worked together on some inventions, particularly the system of conveyance that took products from one process to another on the factory floor.

In creating recipes and food products, my father often experimented with recipes in the kitchen at his office and at home and kept meticulous notes of his cooking experiments. My brother Charles asked me if I remembered the one hundred Mexican rice recipes that we taste-tested. These were cooked in the interest of developing a dried rice mix to be produced by Champion Foods and sold in grocery stores—and also used on the Mexican plate at Casa de Fritos.

Dad's notes for these experiments say, "Took a #10 can of fried rice that Boedecker [the head

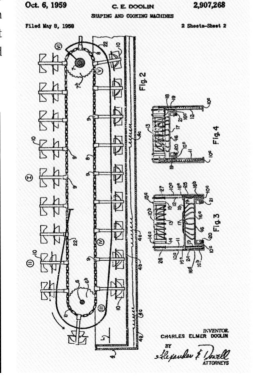

Oct. 6, 1959   C. E. DOOLIN   2,907,268
SHAPING AND COOKING MACHINES
Filed May 8, 1958   2 Sheets-Sheet 2

INVENTOR.
CHARLES ELMER DOOLIN
BY
Alexander & Dowell
ATTORNEYS

◀ The drawing for the Ta-Cup machine patent, dated 1959

Casa de *Fritos.*
AUTHENTIC MEXICAN FOOD

COMBINATION PLATES

1.
6 Tamales,
Rice & Beans
.85

3.
2 Tamales, Rice, Beans,
Salad & Ta-cup
1.00

2.
1 Enchilada,
Rice, Beans, Salad
& Ta-cup
1.00

4.
2 Tamales,
1 Enchilada, Rice, Beans,
Salad & Ta-cup
1.25

A LA CARTE

Ta-cup .30

Refried Beans .25

Spanish Rice .25

Chili & Beans .45

Spaghetti & Chili .40

2 Enchiladas .50

3 Tamales .35

Luncheon Salad .25

Coffee .10

Cold Drinks .10 & .20

Ice Cream .15 & .20

Milk .15

Chalupa "Frijoles in a Ta-cup" .25

FRITOS SERVED WITH ALL DISHES

AS ENJOYED IN DISNEYLAND, U. S. A.

THE *Frito* STORY

It all began back in 1932 when a young Texan, C. E. Doolin, stopped for lunch at a tiny San Antonio cafe. He was intrigued by the dish of chips that came with his meal – chips made from a tortilla, the native corn cake of Mexico. They had been cut into thin strips and fried. And they were mighty delicious.

Sure that others would enjoy his discovery, Mr. Doolin bought the recipe from the cafe owner. Then with the aid of his mother and brother, Mr. Doolin began to produce the chips – right in the family kitchen.

At first, Mr. Doolin made the chips – now known as Fritos – just for neighboring stores and restaurants. But more and more requests from farther and farther away came in for the chips. Soon Mr. Doolin had to move out of the kitchen and open a small plant. As the years passed, the demand for Fritos grew still greater. Today, Fritos plants across the country turn out *millions* of chips each day to satisfy America's love for Fritos!

THE FRITO KID – *one of the star performers at the Casa de Fritos – is the symbol of Fritos – king size or regular. Look for them both at your grocers!*

Menu from Casa de Fritos. "The Frito Story" at lower left is the story of how the company began.

of the Champion Foods division] had prepared for me and put it into an electric fryer in 6 cups of boiling water. . . . Put the finished rice back in the #10 can and found that it had shrunk."

Dad developed a recipe for tortillas, and the tortillas were eventually sold, for a while, as "Fritos Tortillas." I found the notes Dad made while he was learning to make tortillas on his own through trial and error. The notes go into an exhaustive amount of detail. I've included a few lines here to give you the flavor: "Wiped a greasy cloth over the fry pan before putting the uncooked tortilla on it. When tried to get under the tortilla with the spatula found it was sticking to the pan. . . . Raised the fry pan to 250 degrees and added a little flour to stiffen the dough. The next tortilla was a little easier to get under to turn over, but there were some dry spots and the edges began to curl up . . . added water to make a softer dough . . . also raised the pan temperature to 260 degrees. This tortilla was easier to turn and when cooked on both sides had a sort of translucent appearance and although could be rolled to make an enchilada, did not seem to taste done and no browning occurred. . . . The thought occurred that a little sugar added to the dough might cause the tortillas to brown a little while cooking."

I also found Dad's notes about using a "Radarange." Radarange was the name given to the first microwave oven; microwaves were developed by Raytheon and introduced in 1947. Dad had the first Radarange in Dallas. It was kept in his experimental Tex-Mex fast food stand, the Tango Dairy Mart, where my half-brother Ronald worked (see chapter 7, "Ronald"). To me this is proof that Dad was truly on the cutting edge of the Tex-Mex fast food business. In his notes, Dad says about using the Radarange: "Put the plate containing two enchiladas in the Radarange with the plate still inverted over it. Set the timer on high for one minute. At the end of the period, checked the enchilada temperature and they were 185 degrees in the center and 200 degrees on the ends. The plates were hot, but not too hot to handle."

Bruce Lane, a friend of Dad's and the owner of the Dairy Mart chain, called me after the airing of the *Hidden Kitchens* Texas National Public Radio show, "The Birth of the Frito," and told me about how he and Dad developed jalapeño bean dip at our house. The August

Dad's experiment with tortillas promptly became packaged and sold—the Frito Company was now in the tortilla business.

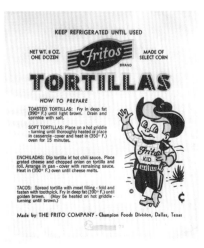

1956 issue of the *Frito Bandwagon* says that bean dip was origi-
nated by William M. Chambers, owner of the Texas Tavern Canning Company. Mr. Chambers became an employee of the Frito
Company through the acquisition of Texas Tavern, as Lamar
Lovvorn, the former treasurer of the Frito Company recently
confirmed for me. I'm guessing that perhaps after Lane and Dad
developed the recipe Chambers put it into production. I also
recently read yet another account of the origin of bean dip in
Robb Walsh's *The Tex-Mex Cookbook*. Walsh writes that Rocky
Rutherford and William Chambers invented the jalapeño bean
dip recipe in 1955. Walsh says that Mr. Rutherford's dip recipe
required a special mash of jalapeños that he fermented in an
oak barrel. This is still the magic of Fritos Bean Dip today. (See
the end of this chapter for a vintage jalapeño bean dip recipe.
Note that today, Fritos Bean Dip has jalepeños in it, though
"Jalepeño" is no longer part of the name. Frito-Lay also markets
an even spicier version, Fritos Hot Bean Dip.)

I recently found, in my father's old wallet, a membership
card dated November 21, 1949. The card is issued to "C. E.
Doolin, a full-fledged and duly qualified life member of the So-
ciété des Gentilshommes Chefs de Cuisine," and is signed in ink
by James Beard, with "Chief Potato Peeler" printed below the

*From left, Uncle Earl, John Campbell,
and Dad in front of the house on the
grounds of the Midlothian Frito farm.*

The Fritos Jalapeno Bean Dip (today simply called "Fritos Bean Dip") featured on this poster was offered to the public as a Fritos product in 1956 when the company purchased 49 percent of Texas Tavern, a canning company.

► *Uncle Earl (right) tells W. M. Wortley, buyer for the Tulsa public school cafeterias, about the old days when the hand-held press—shown here gold-plated and under a glass dome—was used in 1932 to make the first Fritos.*

THE FIRST
Fritos Machinery
The *Original* Hand Press by which the first *Fritos* were manu-factured 21 years ago. In those days it [a] hand [oper...] 240 pkgs. was a [...] days work

▼ *The early hammer press shown in this drawing was developed by Uncle Earl and Dad to extrude and cut Fritos in larger quantities than was possible with the hand-operated machine. This launched the mechanization of Fritos production, but the device still had to be hit manually with a hammer to cut the chip.*

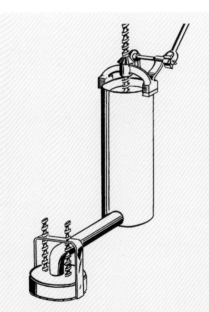

This early Frito press was operated by pulling the lever at top right and then hitting the top of the cutter, at lower left, with a hammer. When hit with the hammer, the cutter snipped the Fritos to the proper length.

It was a common occurence for the cutter to be in the welding shop for repair due to the heavy blows it received with the hammer.

line. Although my father never did any of the family cooking at home, his interest in food and his cooking experiments and nutritional expertise made him well qualified for membership in such a society. I had no idea he considered himself a chef, but he apparently had the James Beard seal of approval.

For a number of years, as we have seen, my Uncle Earl was the head of engineering as well as vice-president of the Frito Company and one of the original co-owners of the Rio Vista farm. He was an inventor in his own right. He successfully patented four inventions, all of them having to do with the manufacturing of Fritos. (My father also patented four inventions.) Uncle Earl's daughter, my cousin Colleen, said that her father's work with the Frito Company made him an expert on corn and potatoes—the way they were processed and their uses. According to Colleen, Uncle Earl turned his inventive nature to cooking after he sold his share of the Frito Company to Dad. He was a meticulous, fastidious, exacting cook who used the scientific method,

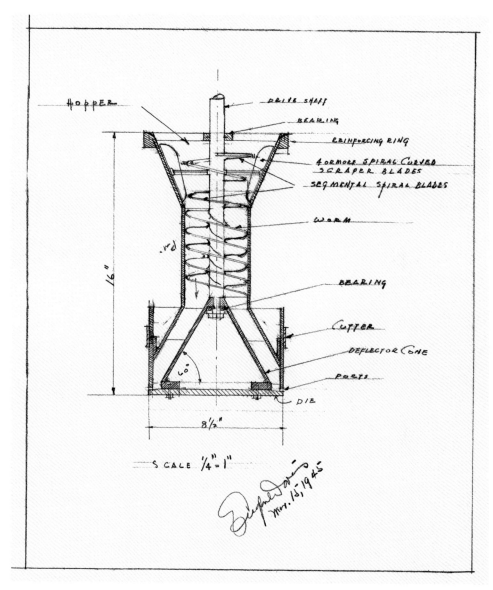

Labels in drawing:

HOPPER — DRIVE SHAFT — BEARING — REINFORCING RING — 4 OR MORE SPIRAL CURVED SCRAPER BLADES — SEGMENTAL SPIRAL BLADES — WORM — BEARING — CUTTER — DEFLECTOR CONE — PORTS — DIE

16"

8½"

SCALE ¼" = 1"

Mechanical drawings for the interior mechanism of the hammer press, by Eugene Davis

making any recipe exactly as it was written—the first time he made it. He figured that would give him a baseline on which to change the ingredients to suit his taste. He developed a corn-bread recipe that used not only his own ingredient proportions but also his own method for preparing the batter. Some of my Uncle Earl's recipes are included here. ∎

Recipes

My cousin Colleen contributed the following recipes, which Uncle Earl loved to make. I wonder whether Uncle Earl might have learned how to make his cornbread from Miss Ferne at the Rio Vista. My Grandpa Coleman loved to turn a glass of milk into dessert by putting sugar and cornbread into it, chopping the cornbread up with a spoon, and eating and slurping the whole thing.

¼ + ¼ cup corn oil
1¾ cups white cornmeal (not
    self-rising)
¼ cup flour
1 tablespoon baking powder
1 teaspoon salt
½ teaspoon soda
½ teaspoon sugar
2 eggs
1½ cups buttermilk

Uncle Earl's Cornbread (vintage)

Contributed by Colleen Jane Doolin Skinner

❖ Pour ¼ cup of the corn oil into a well-seasoned 9-inch iron skillet and heat it in a 350-degree oven until it is hot enough to spit if a few drops of water are sprinkled in it. The oil may be heated on a stove burner, but do not let it smoke. Mix the dry ingredients in a small bowl, using a round whisk. Mix the wet ingredients—the egg, buttermilk, and remaining ¼ cup of corn oil—in a bowl large enough for all the ingredients. After the oil in the skillet is hot—and only then—pour the dry ingredients into the bowl with the wet ingredients; gently mix only until the dry ingredients are moistened, then quickly pour the batter into the heated skillet using a rubber scraper and immediately place in the heated oven. Bake until the top is browned and the sides have pulled away from the skillet, about 25–30 minutes. The cornbread should shake free in the skillet and easily tip onto a plate.

Another of Uncle Earl's recipes is a stew known as "Evelyn." According to Colleen, Uncle Earl, in his prime, was quite the ladies' man (he was married five times), and Evelyn was the first of his wives. This stew appears to have been developed during their relatively brief marriage.

Uncle Earl's Evelyn (vintage)

❖ Fry the ground meat in an iron skillet—no extra oil needed. Add the onion, chopped bell pepper, and celery and sauté until tender. Then add the potatoes, carrots, tomato sauce *or* diced tomatoes, and the water. Simmer until the potatoes and carrots are tender. Then add the corn and mushrooms. Simmer until all the vegetables are done, season as desired, and serve with cornbread.

1½ pounds very lean ground beef or buffalo
½ onion, chopped
1 small bell pepper, chopped
1 stalk celery, chopped
2 potatoes, diced (or substitute a handful of macaroni)
2 small carrots, diced
1 can (15 ounces) tomato sauce *or* diced tomatoes
1½ cans (same 15-ounce can) of water
2 ears of fresh corn, sliced off the cobs
1 box (8 ounces) of fresh mushrooms, sliced
1 tablespoon chili powder (optional)

Uncle Earl's Baked Beans (vintage)

❖ Spray an 8x8-inch pan with cooking spray and add the pork and beans. Cover with the strips of bacon, then spread the ketchup over the bacon and top evenly with the brown sugar. Bake at 350 degrees for an hour or until bubbly around the edges.

1 can (15 ounces) Van Camps Pork and Beans (Colleen said, "Daddy was sometimes brand-specific, and this is the time.")
3 to 4 strips of bacon
½ cup ketchup
½ cup brown sugar
Corn oil cooking spray

Uncle Earl's Texas Chili (vintage)

❖ Heat the oil in a large skillet and cook the meat, stirring constantly, until it is a gray color. Push it to one side and sauté the onion until tender. Add the tomato sauce, spices, and water. Stir until blended, simmering at a low temperature. To quickly and completely dissolve the masa or flour in the ½ cup of water, shake it in a tightly closed jar. Then add the flour-and-water mixture to the skillet and blend. Simmer for about 1½ hours, stirring occasionally. Remove the bay leaf and, if desired, add the pinto beans.

2 teaspoons corn oil
2 pounds top round steak, diced into chili chunks
1 small onion, chopped
1 can (8 ounces) tomato sauce
1 scant teaspoon ground cumin
1 teaspoon paprika
¼ teaspoon cayenne pepper (more for hotter chili, less for milder)
2 teaspoons salt
1 bay leaf
1 tablespoon oregano
¼ teaspoon garlic powder
½ cup chili powder (fresh—homemade if you have it)
1½ cups water
2 tablespoons masa *or* 1 tablespoon flour—dissolved in ½ cup water
2 cups cooked pinto beans (optional)

This recipe uses Fritos bean dip in a casserole. In my reading I've come across the fact that jalapeño bean dip first gained its popularity in bars where it was sold in small five-cent cans to customers as an accompaniment to five-cent bags of Fritos. Even though the name "Fritos Bean Dip" no longer reflects it, jalapeños are still an ingredient, so I've retained the word in the names of two recipes in this chapter.

1 can (10½ ounces) Fritos Bean Dip
1 cup chopped onion
1 can (10½ ounces) condensed tomato soup
1 cup grated sharp American cheese

Jalapeño Bean Dip Casserole (vintage)

❖ Spread a layer of bean dip in a greased 1½-quart casserole. Add the chopped onion and pour the undiluted soup over the bean dip and onion. Sprinkle the grated cheese over the top. Bake at 350 degrees for 45 minutes. Great, of course, eaten along with Fritos. Serves 4.

The other day I created a Southwest-themed turkey loaf with Hatch peppers and crushed Doritos Nacho Cheese Flavored Tortilla Chips. The challenge of making a turkey loaf is that it can be flavorless. I think that my "kitchen sink" approach to flavoring it really works.

1 tablespoon canola oil
1 medium onion, diced
1 egg
1 pound ground turkey
½ cup apple juice
1 tablespoon cornstarch
¼ teaspoon salt
¼ teaspoon ground cumin
Fresh ground pepper
1 can (5¾ ounces) Hatch or other mild chili peppers, drained and diced
1 cup crushed Doritos Nacho Cheese Flavored Tortilla Chips
4 ounces sharp Cheddar cheese, grated

Southwestern Turkey Loaf (original)

By Kaleta Doolin

❖ Preheat the oven to 400 degrees. Heat the canola oil in a small skillet and sauté the onion until it begins to turn clear. In a large mixing bowl, whip the egg until it turns an even lemon yellow. Add the remaining ingredients except for the cheese. Mix well by hand. Roll the mixture into a loaf shape and place it in an oiled loaf pan. Bake at 400 degrees for 45 minutes. Remove from the oven and check the internal temperature for doneness (180 degrees) with a meat thermometer. Cover with the grated cheese and return to the oven for another 5 minutes. Serves 4.

VARIATIONS

❖ Top the meatloaf while baking with Sauce Olé. The cooking time will be about 10 minutes longer. OR, top plated slices of Turkey Meatloaf with Jalapeño Bean Dip Fondue.

1 can (10½ ounces) Fritos Bean Dip (or Hot Bean Dip if you prefer)
1 cup milk

Sauce Olé (vintage)

❖ Blend together the jalapeño bean dip and the milk. Pour over the top of your favorite meat loaf before baking.

1 can (10½ ounces) Fritos Bean Dip
1 cup grated sharp American cheese

Jalapeño Bean Dip Fondue (vintage)

❖ Combine the bean dip with the grated cheese. Heat slowly over low heat until the cheese is melted. Serve hot with Fritos corn chips or Doritos, or pour over plated slices of your favorite meat loaf.

Chapter 7

Ronald

I n January 2008 I took a trip to interview my half-brother Ronald Elmer Doolin. Until then, the last time I had seen Ronald was seven years ago and before that, forty-seven years ago. When I met with him recently, I learned a lot of new things about my father and the history of the Frito Company. I knew before I got together with Ronald that what he had to say would show me the flip side of my father, and I wasn't disappointed.

Ronald in tie and jodhpurs and Charles Bernard Doolin (our paternal grandfather). Both of these snapshots were taken at the family's home at 1416 Roosevelt Avenue in San Antonio.

Ronald, being very much himself in Sacramento

Ronald at military school

Ronald had a checkered past in both military schools he attended as a young man. His beliefs ran contrary to the establishment, but for some unknown reason he ended up joining the navy. In the navy he contracted a rare disease that temporarily paralyzed him—Guillain-Barré syndrome, or chronic inflammatory demyelinating polyneuropathy. This was not the only disease that Ronald contracted in the service. He had also nearly died with encephalitis. After Ronald's recovery from that very serious fight for life in a naval hospital in Philadelphia, Dad did not want him to reenlist and promised to give him a job in the Frito Company, so at the age of twenty-five Ronald moved to Dallas and was put in charge of an experimental restaurant named Tango Dairy Mart.

Dad had opened the Tango Dairy Mart because he wanted to test the concept of a fast food, Dairy Queen-type menu combined with a Mexican food menu. The new food stand would also be a testing ground for Dad's new invention, the Ta-Cup, and its kitchen equipment, the newly minted Radarange microwave.

The menu at Tango Dairy Mart was hamburgers, hotdogs, and tacos in Ta-Cups, along with prepared food items produced by Champion Foods such as tamales and enchiladas. Ronald told me that Dad didn't want him to sell chicken at the Tango Dairy Mart and that he had to lie to Dad about eggs he had in the refrigerator for customers, saying that they were for himself. Ronald was not supposed to make or serve anything other than the menu that Dad set out, but Ronald made egg breakfasts and his own special chicken recipe (given below) for a few of his regulars. He says that he was driven to do this because the Dairy Mart's location in the Gus Thomason and Ferguson Road Casa View shopping center did not have any foot traffic, since the stand was stuck way back

Ronald sent this photo to my parents when he joined the Navy.

in a corner. Therefore, he had to expand Dad's menu to attract and keep repeat customers. (When Ronald and his wife Virginia were in Dallas for my son's graduation, we went to the spot in the Casa View Center where the Tango Dairy Mart had been situated, and I saw that it was indeed a terrible location.)

Ronald said that another problem he had at the fast food stand was that people didn't know how to eat the Ta-Cups that Dad was testing. The Ta-Cups were too small to look good served in a bowl so people had to hold them in their hands. Once the customers took the first bite, Ronald reported, the filling would begin spilling out, which was "real messy" and made it necessary to use a fork to eat the rest. This opinion directly contradicts what my father had to say about Ta-Cups in the December 3, 1958, issue of the *Dallas Times Herald*. In an article headlined "Winter Inspires Open-Face Taco," my father is quoted as saying, "You're supposed to eat a taco with your hands. Now it can be eaten like an open sandwich. The cup won't split and the customer doesn't get the filling all over himself."

Ronald and Dad had a tempestuous relationship. Dad accused Ronald of dipping into the Tango Dairy Mart till, which Ronald flatly denies although he did admit to me that he traded cans of tamales for beer at a local bar. Dad fired Ronald, partly for the discrepancies in the cash register receipts, which may have resulted from Ronald's tamale-for-beer trading. (The fact that Dad even noticed them is a tribute to his strict accounting. I also have letters from Dad to various recipients, alluding to suspicions of theft in other parts of the company, which give further evidence of his thorough knowledge of the company's most minute financial details.) Other reasons for the firing were Tango Dairy Mart's failure and the fact that Ronald had messed up Dad's experiment by deviating from the prescribed menu. This was the first of several occasions when Ronald was fired by Dad. Ronald enumerated each of these occasions when I met with him in Sacramento.

Ronald told me a number of things I had not known about my father. One was that Dad drank alcohol earlier in his life; this came as a surprise to me since I had thought that Dad was always a teetotaler, as he was when I knew him. Ronald also said that Dad was not a strict vegetarian when he was not around my mother and us children, that he would occasionally "cheat" and eat a little meat. He also offered some juicy tidbits about Dad's relationship with his first wife, Ronald's mother, Faye Floree Richards. Ronald said of his mother, "She was a party girl," which leads me to believe that she might have been a heavy drinker or even an alcoholic. He said that Dad caught her having an affair at her father's house in El Reno, Oklahoma (where she grew up and where her family of origin still lived), with a man named Scotty Reese. Dad initiated a divorce and got embroiled in a custody fight over Ronald, which he won. Faye married Scotty.

I also learned some new things about Ronald. Sometime after working at the Tango Dairy Mart, he worked at Champion Foods making tamales. He says

Ronald loved his uniforms as he had loved costumes as a child.

that Dad fired him from that job for missing one day of work when he had to take his wife at that time, Ruth, to a doctor's appointment. The story I had heard about this incident was that Ronald left work against the orders of the manager of Champion Foods, George Boedeker. Mr. Boedeker called Dad to report that Ronald was MIA, and Dad told him to fire Ronald. Apparently, Dad believed in "tough love."

Ronald had married Zella Ruth Young on March 11, 1950. Ruth, as she was always called, had a son Charles ("Chuck") by another marriage. Ronald adopted Chuck and then Ronald and Ruth had a daughter and a son together, Diana Dean (named for Grandmother Daisy Dean Doolin) and Kenneth Richards Doolin.

After Ruth died, Ronald married twice more; his current wife is a very sweet woman named Virginia Doolin.

Ronald told me a dramatic story about a meeting with Dad in the Frito Company lawyer's office that brought about the death of his relationship with Dad. I don't know why they met at the lawyer's office or what precipitated the final interaction. All I know is the picture Ronald painted for me of Dad sitting on a couch in his Humphrey Bogart hat and suit and ordering Ronald "to get out of town." To which Ronald responded, "I don't have enough money to get to the outskirts of Dallas." Ronald told me this story in a funny, tongue-in-cheek tone. He said the whole scene was like something out of a movie.

Ronald says that he invented the first Doritos® by cutting a tortilla into wedges and frying it up at the Tango Dairy Mart.

*Ronald and I getting acquainted
in Sacramento. Ronald told me a
number of things I had not known
about my father.*

*Dad and Ronald standing in front of
a "Frito car" at the house on Roosevelt
Street in San Antonio. You can see the
doorway of the garage that housed
early Frito production after it moved
there from the family kitchen.*

Employees working in the research laboratory at the newly opened California office

He also experimented with different salt flavorings to put on these chips and combined different flavored chips in a bowl to serve his customers, many of whom ordered the flavored chips over and over. Apparently Ronald invented a version of what was eventually called the Dorito, but he probably didn't know how to follow up and his Dorito recipe never made it to Fritos' Research and Development Department. I do recognize Ronald as another third-generation Fritos recipe innovator.

Ronald told me that after Dad died, my mother offered to give him the Tango Dairy Mart stand, but Ronald refused the gift, saying he would need $10,000 to run the business. (I learned recently that another one of Dad's businesses, a hamburger stand called Cheesteak, sold for $13,750 after Dad's death, and that Dixie Enterprises, which probably owned a chain of barbecue drive-ins called Pig Stands, sold for $2,866, but that Tango Enterprises was only valued at $1.)

The Tango Dairy Mart, Cheesteak, and Pig Stands left the Frito Company along with Dad. It was many years before the entity that was Frito-Lay became a part of PepsiCo and the company moved back in the direction of fast-food chains, eventually spinning them all off into a separate company called "Yum." ■

Recipes

Here's the recipe for chicken that Ronald used when he made his bootleg chicken from taco-stand ingredients at the Tango Dairy Mart.

Ronald's Bootleg Chicken (vintage)

1 whole chicken (3½ to 4 pounds)
Mexican sauce (non-specific)
3 cups cooked rice (enough to loosely fill the chicken cavity; this was likely the Fritos brand made by the Champion Foods Division called "Rice N' Spice")

❖ Baste the chicken inside and out with Mexican sauce of some type. Fill the chicken cavity with the rice. Truss the cavity. Place the chicken on its back and bake 30 minutes at 350 degrees, basting once or twice. Then cook it on each side 30 minutes or more until done (total of 1 ½ to 2 hours). Baste often. Cut the chicken in half lengthwise. Ronald's hand written notes say that this makes "perfect servings" for two, but it could serve three or even four.

Next is the recipe for the spices Ronald put on the tortillas he quartered and fried, his early "Doritos."

Ronald's Spiced Chips (vintage)

1 tablespoon oregano flakes
4 tablespoons salt
2 teaspoons pepper
2 teaspoons monosodium glutamate (optional)
4 teaspoons garlic powder
Corn tortillas
Oil for deep frying

❖ Mix well. Allow to set 2–5 days before using. Toss with hot tortilla chips fresh from the fryer.

Here's another recipe for chicken using Fritos corn chips. It was developed by Nell Morris, aka "Daisy Dean," the Fritos marketing character tradename.

Fritos Mexican Chicken Appetizer (vintage)

2 cups + ½ cup Fritos corn chips
1 medium onion, chopped
1 clove garlic, minced
1 cup cooked chicken, chopped or sliced
1 cup grated American cheese
1 can (14 ounces) condensed tomato soup diluted with ½ cup water
1 teaspoon chili powder

❖ Place the 2 cups of corn chips in a 2-quart casserole. Arrange a layer over the corn chips using half of the chopped onion, minced garlic, chicken, and grated cheese. Repeat the layer using the other half of the same ingredients. Mix the diluted soup with the chili powder, heat, and pour over the ingredients in the casserole. Top with the remaining corn chips and cheese. Bake at 350 degrees for 15–20 minutes. Serves 6–8.

Chapter 8

Fritos Chili Pie®

ACCORDING TO a newspaper article published in the 1960s, "While recipes are created for Frito-Lay's entire line of snack products and canned foods, perhaps the most famous recipe developed by the Consumer Service department is that for Fritos Chili Pie."

Fritos Chili Pie, still one of the better-known Frito recipes and a traditional comfort food in the Southwest, is not a pie *per se*. The basic Frito pie simply consists of Fritos corn chips, chili, onions, and cheese. Any variations in the recipe usually involve the placement and texture of the Fritos and even the vessel in which the "pie" is made. Sometimes it's prepared as a casserole or started in a Crockpot, but sometimes it's prepared directly in a cardboard boat or, famously in the past, when the bags were sturdier, in the Fritos bags themselves. Some recipes are in bulk. The variations are endless, and some by contemporary

This Fritos Chili Pie point-of-sale handout was for distributors. It was designed to make the distributors aware of marketing options and also to educate them in aggressive marketing.

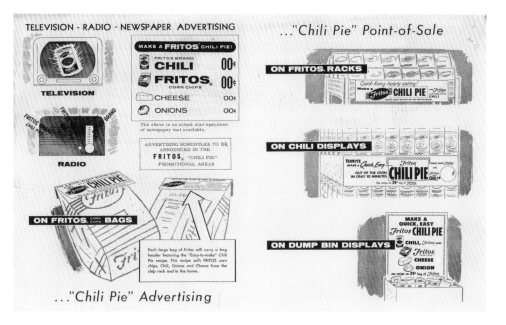

This Fritos Chili Pie seasonal ad was aimed at "winter appetites."

chefs are quite complex. The recipes at the end of this chapter are samples from across this range.

Fritos Chili Pie was one of the first recipes given away at conventions as part of the Cooking with Fritos promotional campaign. It was chosen for this purpose because it used (and therefore sold) two Fritos products: Fritos corn chips and Fritos Brand Chili. The chili was produced by the company's Champion Foods division. In his book *Bowl of Red,* Frank X. Tolbert

Fritos® hili Pie

included Fritos Brand Chili in a list of canned chilies he considered admirable because they followed classic recipes.

Fritos Chili Pie was also featured in point-of-sale marketing displays in grocery stores, where copies of the recipe were available along with cans of chili and small bags of Fritos. (Originally all Fritos were sold in small 5-cent bags, then later in slightly larger 15-cent bags; "economy size" bags didn't come till much later.) In 1962, during the company's sixth annual

This poster picturing a Fritos Chili Pie Casserole was displayed with Fritos products in grocery stores. Point-of-sale advertising (that is, putting ads where products were sold) was pioneered by the Frito Company. So were incentive programs, appeals to seasonal appetites, and other marketing tools.

Chili Pie promotion, over one million bag headers, folded over the top of Fritos bags and stapled, carried the recipe. The recipe given away in grocery stores and at conventions said, "Heat can of chili, pour into bag of Fritos, and sprinkle with grated cheese and chopped onions."

This concoction was popular at football games because it could easily be produced at snack bars and handed to customers

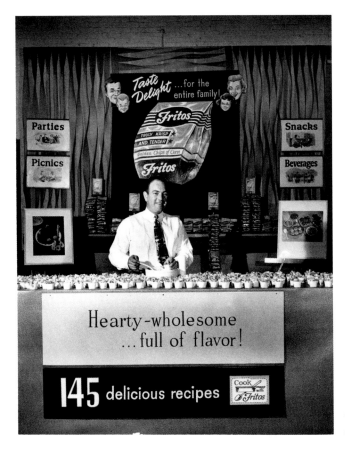

Fritos Chili Pie samples offered at a convention

along with plastic spoons to scoop up every bit of chili, cheese, and Fritos from the bag. Many people have told me that they have fond memories of eating Fritos Chili Pie during their high school football games. It also was and continues to be a favorite at drive-in restaurants such as Sonic, and at baseball parks, Cub Scout meetings, state and county fairs, rodeos, fundraisers, open houses, and bingo games. It has reached the status of comfort food, at least in Texas.

In the 1960s Teresa Hernandez popularized the Fritos Chili Pie at Woolworth's—later the Five & Dime General Store—in Santa Fe, New Mexico, using her mother's recipe for red chili. She refused to add any garnishes, saying that the original recipe didn't use lettuce or tomato. Hernandez is quoted on the Internet as saying, "The trick is to get the chili in the bag. But if you love what you're doing, everything will come out good." At one point she sold as many as fifty-six thousand Fritos Chili Pies in one year.

The tie-in to popular TV shows for kids helped promote Fritos as a kid food.

Many people have the misconception that Teresa Hernandez invented the Fritos Chili Pie recipe, but it was on the menu of the Dallas Dietetic Association's 1949 closing banquet and was already widespread in grocery stores as early as 1956, well before it was printed on those million bag headers in 1962. I'm not sure whether Mother Doolin or Mary Livingston, Dad's executive secretary, invented the recipe. Maybe neither did and the recipe was invented by Nell Morris when the Frito Company acquired the Champion Chili Company in 1952, and it seemed like a good idea to distribute a simple recipe that included both Fritos and chili. The company itself credits the recipe for Fritos Chili Pie to Nell Morris, but I find evidence that it came before she was hired.

This bag header points out the ingredients for a basic Fritos Chili Pie. The recipe given away in grocery stores and at conventions was equally simple: Heat can of chili, pour into bag of Fritos, and sprinkle with grated cheese and chopped onions.

When Fritos Chili Pie is made as a casserole it's layered, with crushed Fritos on the bottom, followed by half of the chili and a layer of cheese and onions, then more crushed Fritos and another layer of chili topped with cheese and onions, with crushed Fritos on top. The casserole comes out of the oven hot and bubbling and, because of the proportion of Fritos to chili, a little crunchy. The first recipe in the group below may be the recipe that was printed on the headers on the Fritos bags distributed in 1962. ■

Recipes

Fritos Chili Pie (vintage)

❖ Reserve some of the corn chips for a topping; place half of the rest in the bottom of a casserole. Pour half the chili over the corn chips. Top with half of the chopped onion and cheese. Repeat, and then top with the corn chips you reserved. Bake at 350 degrees for 20 minutes or until well heated and the onion is thoroughly cooked. Serves 4–6.

2 cups lightly crushed Fritos corn chips
1 can chili (without beans)
1 large onion, chopped
1 cup grated American cheese

Fritos Chili Pie for 50 (vintage)

This recipe calls for chili from scratch, but if you prefer, you can use 8 No. 2 cans of chili instead. You'll need to puree them. Serve on a divided lunch tray with other side dishes.

❖ Soak the pinto beans in water for 8 hours. When they appear to be their original size and are plump, cover them with water and cook until tender. Then puree them and set them aside.

    Next, make chili out of the next 7 ingredients (unless you are using canned chili): Render the suet in a pan and then remove the suet fiber. Brown the garlic cloves in this fat, and then re-move them. Add the ground chili pepper pods, chili powder, ground beef, and tomato puree. Simmer for 20 minutes or until the beef is tender. Add salt to taste.

    Mix the chili with the pureed beans. Place 2 pounds of the crushed corn chips in the bottom of a 20x12x2-inch pan. Pour the chili mixture over the chips. Sprinkle with diced onions and grated cheese. Sprinkle the other ½ pound of chips on top of this layer. Bake at 350 degrees for 30 minutes.

1½ pounds dried pinto beans
½ pound suet
2 cloves garlic
2 ounces chili pepper pods, ground
1 ounce (4 tablespoons) chili powder
3 pounds ground beef
1¾ quarts tomato puree
    Salt to taste
2 + ½ pounds Fritos corn chips, crushed
1 pound onions, chopped
1 pound American cheese, grated

Fritos Pie in the Bag (vintage)

❖ Mix together the yellow cornmeal, chili powder, black pepper, cumin, salt, fresh oregano, and red pepper flakes. Place the mixture in a skillet over medium heat and. toast for seven min-utes. Remove from heat.

    Brown the ground beef and brisket cubes in another skillet. Drain and set aside. In a large Dutch oven or 6-quart stock ▶

3 tablespoons yellow cornmeal
3 tablespoons chili powder
2 teaspoons black pepper
1 teaspoon cumin
1 teaspoon salt
1 teaspoon oregano (fresh)
½ teaspoon red pepper flakes
1 pound lean ground beef
1½ pounds beef brisket, cubed
3 cups chopped onion
2 tablespoons oil
3 cloves garlic, chopped
1 can (28 ounces) chopped tomatoes
1 can (10¾ ounces) tomato puree
12 ounces beer (preferably Mexican or Texas lager)
1 cup water
24 small bags of Fritos corn chips
6 ounces grated Cheddar cheese (optional)
Green onions, chopped, for garnish (optional)

▶▶ pot, sauté the chopped onion in the 2 tablespoons of oil until transparent. Add the ground beef, brisket cubes, and chopped garlic. Then add the toasted spices, canned chopped tomatoes, tomato puree, beer, and water. Simmer stirring frequently on low heat for 1 hour. Open each bag and spoon the chili over the corn chips. Top each serving with grated Cheddar cheese and chopped green onions. Serves 24.

---

3 pounds lean ground meat
3 cloves garlic, minced
1 large onion, chopped
¾ cup dry beans (or 1 15-ounce can of pinto beans)
4 cups water (reduce to 1½ to 2 cups if using canned beans)
1 teaspoon salt
1 envelope taco seasoning
1 package (15 ounces) Fritos corn chips
2 tomatoes, diced
3 cups Monterey Jack and Cheddar cheese, shredded
16 ounces salsa
16 ounces sour cream
Preserved jalapeño slices

Crockpot Fritos Pie (contemporary)

Start this recipe in your slow cooker in the morning and in the afternoon, you'll be all ready to assemble your pies with homemade chili.

❖ In a Crockpot, combine the meat, garlic, onion, beans, water, salt, and taco seasoning. . Stir well. Cover and cook on high for 8–10 hours. Serve on individual plates with a bed of corn chips on each one. Top with diced tomatoes, shredded cheese, salsa, a dollop of sour cream, and jalapeños.

My tastes have evolved to prefer a heavier flavoring than the previous taco-like Crockpot pie. Here is a new version with newer tastes for you to try.

Spray vegetable or canola oil
½ chopped onion
3 cloves garlic, minced
1½ pound lean ground grass-fed beef
2 cups water
1 can (8-ounce) tomato sauce
Wick Fowler's Texas One-Step Chili Seasoning Mix
Beans (drained and washed; optional)

Kaleta's 2010 Crockpot Chili (original)

By Kaleta Doolin

❖ Spray the bottom of the skillet with vegetable or canola oil. Add the onion and garlic and cook. Add the meat and chop into small pieces with a spoon. Turn until meat is browned. Empty the skillet into the Crockpot. Add the remaining ingredients and cook on the low setting for 8–10 hours.

Dean Fearing, the well-known chef at Fearing's Restaurant in the Dallas Ritz-Carlton hotel, makes innovative Texan cuisine. He sent me a contemporary recipe for Fritos Chili Pie. The recipe uses Cos's Chili—Dean named it after Bill Cosby because it's Cosby's favorite chili. Instead of using Fritos the recipe calls for fried strips of thin tortillas. The chili is made with diced sirloin. The whole concoction is garnished with a colorful sprinkling of grated Cheddar cheese, minced fresh jalapeños, and minced red onion. And, though this is definitely a gourmet approach, as a nod to the original Fritos Chili Pie concept, the dish is served in a Dixie cup.

Dean's Fritos Pie with Cos's Chili

By Chef Dean Fearing

Before putting together your Frito Pie, you'll need to fry up some tortilla strips, toast chilies, and make a chili paste, and then a fine homemade chili. You'll find this pie to be worth making again and again. You can get 100 5-ounce Dixie cups in a pack.

Here are the ingredients and method for each step:

FIRST, FRY THE TORTILLA STRIPS:

❖ In a medium sauté pan heat canola oil to 350 degrees. Add the tortilla strips and cook until crispy. Remove from oil and place on paper towels to drain excess oil. Season with salt.

1	quart canola oil
5	yellow corn tortillas, cut into short, narrow strips

NEXT, TOAST THE CHILIES:

❖ Remove stems and seeds from the chilies and put them into a 350-degree oven for about 1 minute.

10	ancho chilies
2	pasilla chilies

NOW USE THE TOASTED CHILIES TO MAKE THE CHILI PASTE:

❖ In a medium sauté pan over medium-high heat add the oil, onion, carrot, shallot, garlic, celery, and jalapeño. Sauté until the vegetables begin to caramelize. Stir in the toasted chilies. Deglaze the mixture with the beer, orange juice, and chicken stock. Cook for another 5 minutes over medium-high heat. Turn the fire down to a simmer, add the peanuts, and cook the mixture until the liquid is reduced by half, about 30 minutes. Puree in a blender until very smooth. ▶

1	tablespoon olive oil
½	small yellow onion, roughly chopped
1	medium carrot, peeled and roughly chopped
1	medium shallot, roughly chopped
3	medium cloves of garlic, smashed
1	rib of celery (leaves removed), chopped
2	jalapeños, sliced
	The chilies you have toasted
1	Shiner Bock beer
1	cup orange juice
1	cup rich chicken stock
¼	cup toasted unsalted peanuts

1 tablespoon olive oil
1¾ pounds sirloin, diced small
1 small yellow onion, chopped
3 cups of the chili paste you
 made
 Salt to taste
 Freshly ground black pepper
 to taste
½ teaspoon cumin
1 teaspoon Tabasco
1 lime, juiced
 Chipotle chilies, pureed
 (optional)

 The tortilla chips you fried
 The chili you made
 Grated cheddar cheese
 Minced fresh jalapeños
 Minced red onions

▶▶ Finally for the heart of the dish.

MAKE THE COS'S CHILI:

❖ Heat the olive oil in a medium sauté pan. Add the meat and on-ions and cook over high heat until the onions turn translucent. Add the chili paste you made and continue to cook over me-dium heat until the meat is tender, about 1 hour. Then season with salt and black pepper to taste and add the cumin, Tobasco sauce, and lime juice. (To make the chili hotter, add chipotle puree to taste.)

OKAY, NOW ASSEMBLE THE PIES:

❖ Put the tortilla strips into Dixie Cups. Spoon chili on top and add grated cheese, minced jalapeños, and onions as desired.

The Stephan Pyles Restaurant is another of my favorite places to eat in Dallas. Here's one of Stephan's recipes for chili from his cookbook The New Texas Cuisine.

¼ cup vegetable oil
4 pounds round steak or well
 trimmed chuck, coarsely
 ground
1 large onion, chopped
2 large cloves garlic, minced
2 teaspoons oregano, minced
1 teaspoon ground cumin
2 tablespoons pure chili powder
6 large ripe tomatoes, blanched,
 peeled, seeded, and diced
3 tablespoons tomato paste
2 cups hot water, brown veal
 stock, or chicken stock
 Salt to taste

Stephan Pyles Pedernales River Chili

❖ Heat the oil in a heavy pan over medium heat. Add the steak, onion, and garlic and cook until lightly browned. Add the remaining ingredients except for the salt and bring to a boil. Lower the heat and simmer uncovered for about 1 hour. Skim occasionally. Season with salt. Serves 8–10.

Frank X. Tolbert Jr., son of the famous Texas historian Frank X. Tolbert Sr., is a well-known chili cook and Texas artist. He is now producing his father's famous "Bowl of Red" chili at the rate of 1,600 pounds per day for the Whole Foods grocery chain. It's an excellent traditional chili and as such doesn't contain beans (the original Fritos Chili Pie used chili without beans), and I find it the easiest chili to use when I want to make Fritos Pie in a hurry. (Frank recently told me that goat Cheddar and red onion add a great new twist to the toppings.) Here's the original Tolbert Sr. recipe.

Jolbert's Original Texas Chili

Puree the chilies in a blender with a tiny bit of their cooking liquid to make a smooth thin paste (use as little liquid as possible, unless you want the chili to be soupy). Return them to the pot in which they were boiled. Render the suet in a pan and then remove the suet fiber. In a large skillet, braise the beef with half the rendered suet. Sprinkle with some of the garlic and onion if desired. When the meat is gray, pour the liquid off into the chili pot with the pureed peppers. Add the remaining suet to the skillet and continue to braise the meat until brown and almost dry; then add the meat to the chili pot and simmer for 30 minutes. Add the remaining ingredients, using the Masa Harina or cornmeal to thicken. Simmer for another 30 minutes or until the meat is very tender. (For a hotter chili, add extra ancho chilies that have been stemmed and seeded but not chopped.) Let the chili rest overnight, if possible, and skim off the excess fat in the morning. Heat and serve.

The next recipe calls for curry paste that you can make yourself if you are sufficiently ambitious. Instructions for it appear at the end of this recipe.

3 to 6 dried ancho chilies, boiled 5 minutes (with a bit of the water reserved), cooled, stemmed, seeded, and chopped (can prepare extra chopped chilies to add at end)
3 pounds lean chuck, cut into bite-sized pieces
2 ounces sweet beef kidney suet (or substitute vegetable oil)
2 to 4 minced garlic cloves, to taste
Chopped onion, to taste
1 tablespoon crushed cumin seed
1 teaspoon oregano
½ cup paprika
1 tablespoon cayenne pepper
1 tablespoon Tabasco sauce
2 tablespoons Masa Harina or cornmeal
1 sprig fresh cilantro, crushed (optional)

Massaman Curry with Beef

By Frito-Lay Executive Chef Stephen Kalil

If you are making your own massaman curry paste, do that first. Otherwise, begin by dry-frying the cinnamon stick, cardamom seeds, and cloves in a saucepan or wok over a low heat. Stir all the ingredients around for 2 to 3 minutes or until fragrant. Remove from the pan.

Heat the oil in the same pan and stir-fry 2 tablespoons of the massaman paste over a medium heat for 2 minutes or until fragrant.

Add the beef to the pan and stir for 5 minutes. Add the coconut milk, stock, ginger, fish sauce, palm sugar, the remaining curry paste, and the peanuts, tamarind puree, and dry-fried spices. Reduce the heat to low and simmer gently for 50–60 minutes, until the meat is tender. Taste, then adjust the seasoning if necessary. Spoon over Fritos in a serving bowl and garnish with chopped green onions. Serves 4. ▶

2 pieces of cinnamon stick
10 cardamom seeds
5 cloves
2 tablespoons vegetable oil
2 + 2 tablespoons massaman curry paste (see recipe below *or* use store-bought paste)
1¾ pounds beef flank rump steak, cut into 2-inch cubes
2 cups coconut milk
1 cup beef stock
2 tablespoons minced ginger
3 tablespoons fish sauce
3 tablespoons palm sugar
¼ cup roasted salted peanuts, without skin
3 tablespoons tamarind puree
Fritos corn chips
Chopped green onions for garnish

2	dried long red chilies, each about 5 inches
1	lemon grass stalk, white part only, finely sliced
1	-inch piece of galangal, finely chopped
5	cloves
4	-inch piece of cinnamon stick, crushed
10	cardamom seeds
½	teaspoon freshly grated nutmeg
6	garlic cloves, finely chopped
4	Asian shallots, finely chopped
4	to 5 coriander (cilantro) roots, finely chopped
1	teaspoon shrimp paste

▶▶ MASSAMAN CURRY PASTE

❖ Remove the stems from the chilies and slit the chilies lengthwise with a sharp knife. Discard the seeds and soak the chilies in hot water for 1 or 2 minutes or until soft. Drain and roughly chop.

Using a mortar and pestle, pound the chilies, lemon grass, galangal, cloves, cinnamon, cardamom seeds, and nutmeg into a paste. (Alternatively, you can use a food processor or blender to grind or blend all the ingredients into as smooth a paste as possible, add cooking oil, as needed.) Add the garlic, shallots, and coriander roots. Pound and mix together. Add the shrimp paste and pound until the mixture is a smooth paste. Makes 1 cup.

Use as required or keep in an airtight jar. The paste will keep for two weeks in the refrigerator and for two months in a freezer.

And finally, here's my recipe for Venison Chili, which I devised with Personal Chef Jennifer McKinney.

2	tablespoons canola oil
1¾	pounds venison, coarsely ground
2	onions (chopped)
1	poblano pepper, chopped
1	green bell pepper, chopped
4	cloves garlic, minced
1	can (16 ounces) whole peeled tomatoes, drained, seeded, and chopped
2	tablespoons chili powder
1½	teaspoons Mexican oregano
1½	teaspoons ground cumin
¾	teaspoon ancho chili powder
¾	teaspoon guajillo chili powder
1	bay leaf
1	teaspoon dark brown sugar
1	bottle (12 ounces) Shiner Bock dark beer
1	cup beef broth
	Salt and pepper to taste

Venison Chili (original)

By Kaleta Doolin and Chef Jennifer McKinney

❖ Heat the oil in a large, heavy pan. Add the venison and brown lightly—about 5 minutes. Add the onions, poblano, bell pepper, and garlic. Stir until the vegetables are almost soft, about 20 minutes. Add the tomatoes, oregano, cumin, all the spices, the sugar, beer, and beef broth. Simmer for 45 minutes. Season with salt and pepper. (As a variation, you can add pinto beans or kidney beans, although Texans usually don't.)

Chapter 9
Natural Hygiene

D AD HAD a weak heart and sought out the advice of Dr. Herbert M. Shelton rather than follow the American Medical Association's prescribed practices. Shelton graduated from the American School of Naturopathy with two doctoral degrees—one in naturopathy and one in naturopathic literature. He also got a doctor of chiropractic degree from the American School of Chiropractic. During the late 1940s Dr. Shelton's natural health philosophy was considered an alternative to the AMA's advice by many people; but by the late 1950s, following the success of the wonder drugs penicillin and other antibiotics, the AMA had overpowered the natural health movement, making its own methods standard practice in this country.

Dad in his youth. Everyone always said he had kind eyes.

Shelton was the author of *Fasting Can Save Your Life,* among other books. In his books, he outlines various health-fostering practices, including how to find health through nutrition. He maintains that toxins build up in the body starting with the first diaper rash. His nationally known clinic, opened in 1928, was located in San Antonio.

Dad was a devout believer in Shelton's philosophy. He stayed in Shelton's clinic on numerous occasions, where he fasted and followed other natural practices prescribed to improve his poor health. My mother also spent time in the clinic. At one point she was diagnosed with breast cancer and purportedly was cured by a stay there. I recently learned that the Frito Company's first treasurer, Emil Jurica, and my Grandmother Doolin also went to the clinic occasionally to heal by fasting.

Shelton was a frequent keynote speaker at

Mom and Dad in high style, circa 1947. Mom had just completed a fast at the Shelton Clinic in San Antonio and though thin and weak still looks like she stepped out of a Vogue *magazine.*

the Natural Food Association (NFA) conventions that my family and I attended every year. We always drove to the conventions, held all around the country, because flying could have affected Dad's heart. I remember going to one in St. Louis, Missouri, and to another in Louisville, Kentucky. The conventions were very hard for restless kids to sit through. Even now I find listening to the recorded keynote speeches excruciating, although they do have some amusing antiquated language. Dad tape-recorded many of Dr. Shelton's speeches, and I recently had them transferred from reel-to-reel tapes onto CDs. It turns out that recordings of Shelton's speeches are rare, according to the Kitchen Sisters, who ended up using a clip from my CD during their *Hidden Kitchens* Texas episode, "Birth of the Frito," after a search for another source of Shelton's speeches turned up nothing.

I didn't realize until I reviewed some of the family archives that so many of our "hygiene" practices were dictated by Dr. Shelton's teachings. I was also surprised to learn that there were several other NFA convention speakers whose wisdom Dad recorded, including Dr. Joseph A. Coconnuer, Dr. Ehrenfried Pfeiffer, and Mrs. Betty Pettit. I wonder if Mom ever mixed up their teachings and attributed their ideas to Dr. Shelton.

Sometimes Mom was a little overboard in her reverence for Dr. Shelton's teachings. On one occasion, while we were staying in St. Louis during one of the many Natural Food Association conventions that we attended, Mom bought a lot of raw foods and made the bureau in our hotel room into our kitchen. According to Mom, one woman at the convention was so concerned that she didn't see us in the dining room that Mom brought her up to our room and showed her our drawer full of raw foods, which allayed the woman's fear that we kids were being starved.

My brothers and sister and I were constantly exposed to information about nutrition; if not being taught by Dr. Shelton himself at the conventions, we were taught by Mom and Dad. We were extremely sheltered and closely supervised. My first experience of freedom was playing in the hallways of a convention hotel with my new friend, Janet Lennon, of the Lennon Sisters, who appeared regularly on the Lawrence Welk show. The Lennon Sisters were at the convention—I don't remember which convention it was—to perform at the closing banquet. In the hallways Janet and I tried to sell pink and purple, rose- and lilac-scented glycerin soaps, made for the NFA fundraiser, to passers-by. This was my first sales experience.

Our family was vegetarian and ate raw food long before it became popular. Mother told us over and over about how much more nutritious food is before it is cooked. I learned that boiling carrots ruins the nutritional value because the vitamins in them are water-soluble. My mother always steamed them. Other vegetables, like potatoes, have most of their vitamins just under the skin and should not be peeled. We always ate the skins of our baked potatoes last with a pat of butter rolled up inside of them; this felt like a real treat. Apple skins, on the other hand, are rough on the lining of the stomach and should be pared off as thinly as possible.

My siblings and I always learned the nutritional values and vitamin contents of everything that went into our bodies. Mom never liked tomatoes because she thought they caused her arthritis to flare up. She also emphasized that we should be very careful not to eat the eyes that grow on potatoes. She would carefully dig the eyes out with the tip of a potato peeler and taught me how to do that, too. She taught me that potatoes, tomatoes, sweet and hot peppers, and eggplant are classified as nightshade foods. The alkaloids in these foods can adversely impact nerve, muscle, and digestive function and may affect joint function as well. Green and sprouted spots on potatoes usually reflect high alkaloid content. (Mom said this was poison.) We did have eggplant casserole on occasion, even though eggplant is a nightshade.

We always had romaine lettuce on our sandwiches but often ate quartered heads of iceberg lettuce for our salads. (Back then it wasn't known that iceberg lettuce has almost zero nutritional value.) Our mixed salads were made up of unusual combinations of raw food. Crookneck yellow squash and zucchini were regulars and green beans (my least favorite) were sometimes thrown in. I didn't know anyone else as a kid who had avocado

▼ *A bag header that was attached to king-size bags of Fritos in the 1960s. Bag headers had visual triggers that made for really effective advertising. This one is both mouthwatering and seasonal.*

© 1959 Fritos is a registered trademark of The Frito Company.

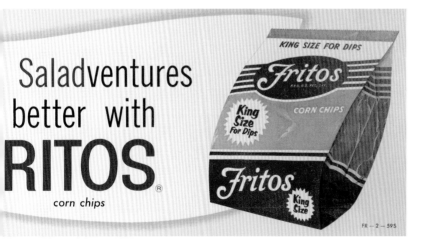

FRITOS CHOCOLATE COOKIES

⅓ cup Butter or Margarine	⅛ tsp. Salt
1 Square Chocolate	1 tsp. Vanilla
½ cup Sugar	½ cup Crushed FRITOS
1 Egg	(measured after crushing)
¼ cup Flour (unsifted, enriched all-purpose)	

Melt butter or margarine and chocolate in double boiler. Add sugar, egg, flour, salt and vanilla. Pour in greased pan 6½"x10½". Sprinkle with FRITOS. Bake at 400 degrees for 12 minutes. Cut in squares. Makes 24 cookies.

FRITOS SMOKE FLAVORED SARDINE SPREAD

1 pkg. (3 oz.) Chive Cream Cheese (room temperature)
1 pkg. (3 oz.) Cream Cheese (room temperature)
6 tbsp. Sour Salad Cream
2 tbsp. Ground or Minced Ripe Olives
¼ tsp. Salt
¼ tsp. Monosodium Glutamate
1 tsp. Lemon Juice
8-10 Smoke Flavored Sardine Fillets (cut in pieces)
3 tbsp. Finely Crushed FRITOS (measured after crushing)

Blend the cheese with the sour cream. Add olives, seasonings, sardines and crushed Fritos. Spread on finger strips of toasted bread. Makes about 25 strips.

FRITOS YUM-YUMS

¾ cup Pitted Dates
3 tbsp. Peanut Butter
⅓ cup Finely Crushed FRITOS (measured after crushing)

Cut dates into fine pieces. Blend with peanut butter. Form into balls the size of a walnut. Roll in crushed FRITOS and serve. Makes 18 small balls.

FRITOS CHOCOLATE CRUNCHIES

For munching after the game and at TV-time, FRITOS Chocolate Crunchies are wonderful! Simply add crushed FRITOS to melted chocolate, drop by spoonfuls on waxed paper, chill and serve.

A Fritos recipe book open to show some of the recipes developed by Nell Morris. The illustrations were by the

CASSEROLE DISHES

QUICK • EASY • DELICIOUS
ONE - DISH MEALS

FRITOS CHICKEN CASSEROLE

1 Hen (average)
1 can Condensed Cream of Mushroom Soup
2 cups FRITOS

Cook hen and bone. Alternate layers of FRITOS and chicken in a casserole. Dilute soup with equal amount of water. Pour over above mixture. Bake at 425 degrees for 30 minutes. Serves 8.

FRITOS CHEESE AND CORN CASSEROLE

2 Strips Bacon
½ Medium Onion (chopped)
1 can (1⅔ cup) Whole Kernel Corn (drained)
½ cup Grated Cheese
¾ tsp. Salt
¼ tsp. Black Pepper

1 cup White Sauce
(3 tbsp. Butter or Margarine
3 tbsp. Flour
1 cup Milk)
1 cup FRITOS crumbs
(measured after crushing)

Fry bacon until crisp. Saute onions in bacon fat, add corn, seasonings, minced bacon, sauce, cheese, and ½ cup FRITOS. Pour into casserole. Sprinkle with remaining FRITOS and bake at 350 degrees for 25 minutes. Serves 6.

FRITOS STUFFED EGGPLANT

1 Eggplant
½ cup Water
½ tsp. Salt
1 Medium Onion (chopped)
2 strips Bacon
1 Egg (hard cooked)

1 tbsp. Bacon Fat
⅛ tsp. White Pepper
2 cups FRITOS crushed lightly (measure after crushing)
¼ cup FRITOS crumbs (measure after crushing)

Cut eggplant lengthwise and scoop out the center, leaving a ½-inch shell. Place in hot salty water for 10 minutes and drain. Cook pulp, onions and salt in water until tender. Fry bacon crisp, mince. To the pulp add 1 tbsp. of bacon fat, minced bacon, chopped eggs, pepper and crushed FRITOS. Fill shells and top with crushed FRITOS. Bake at 350 degrees for 30 minutes. Serves 6.

Glenn Advertising Agency.

Why doesn't she do this more often?

and sprout sandwiches in their lunch bags. We never used canned foods except for Campbell's cream of mushroom soup concentrate, and Chicken of the Sea tuna. We did occasionally eat frozen foods, which Mom said were a step above canned food of any sort. I remember that we used to have frozen baby lima beans and frozen peas. We also made our own creamed corn in large quantities; most of it was frozen so we could eat it later on. I sat and watched our governess, Verna Johnson, while she spent hours grating every last morsel of corn off the cobs in preparation for making creamed corn.

Our childhood was filled with health-food-store items like "Vege-Sal," which was a dried vegetable mixture made with dehydrated celery and used as a salt substitute (because Dr. Shelton said that salt was a poison). We were given raw sugar, honey, cashew butter, seven-grain cereal, whole wheat bread, and fresh figs and ground dates rolled in coconut. Many of these foods, such as figs and olives, were unusual at the time, and I was sometimes teased by my schoolmates when I would take them out of my sack lunch.

Dr. Shelton was like a guru to my mom and dad. He told his followers about how to care for their bodies in every way. *Every* way. In listening to the recordings of his speeches recently, I'm reminded of all the natural hygiene instructions Mom taught us throughout our childhood and adolescence. Not only did Dr. Shelton preach about "proper nutrition," he also added dictums on almost every aspect of life, including such things as proper elimination, "sexual correctness" (see Volume 5 of Dr. Shelton's opus, *The Hygienic System*), and the correct water temperature for bathing. (During one lecture Dr. Shelton went into an agitated tirade—you can almost picture him jumping up and down—about people taking boiling hot baths and coming out like lobsters; he added more calmly that we should always bathe only in lukewarm water.) He also proclaimed that putting anything through your skin by injection was "a crime against life." He may have been partially right about that, since many people are now saying that vaccinations containing mercury may cause autism, and people getting flu shots are asked to sign disclaimers warning that in rare instances they could contract Guillian-Barré syndrome, the same disease my half-brother Ronald has.

When I got married my mother gave me a little chapbook written by Dr. Shelton. Published in 1951 by "Dr. Shelton's Health School," it's called *Food Combining Made Easy*. In it, Dr. Shelton discusses how various food groups shouldn't be eaten at the same time, and how liquids should be taken before or after, but not during, meals, for optimal digestion. According to Dr. Shelton, "If [water is] taken with meals, it dilutes the digestive juices and then passes out of the stomach in short order carrying the digestive juices and their enzymes along with it."

Dr. Shelton's encyclopedic seven-volume work mentioned above—*The Hygienic System*—was first published in 1934 and reprinted on several occasions. Titles of individual volumes include *Orthobionomics* (economics of correct living), *Orthotrophy* (nutrition and food combining), *Fasting, Orthokinesiology* (corrective exercise), *Orthogenetics* (sexual correctness), *Diseases,* and *Orthopathy* (correction of specific diseases). Dr. Shelton also published books entitled *Syphilis: Werewolf of Medicine* and *The Exploitation of Human Suffering*.

These days I hear echoes of Dr. Shelton wherever I turn. Food combining has resurfaced, and people are fasting, eating raw food, and emphasizing eating fresh foods grown locally, all of which Shelton advocated in his day. Like my father, he was ahead of his time.

After my father died, my mother donated a significant amount of money to Dr. Shelton's cause because my father believed so strongly in what Shelton preached. In the dedication to his 1961 book *Rubies in the Sand,* Dr. Shelton wrote, "To Charles Elmer Doolin (deceased) and his wife Mary Kathryn Doolin, whose munificence made possible the erection of the new *Dr. Shelton's Health School,* a modern temple of *Natural Hygiene* where no magic of the shaman, no flumdummery of the priesthood and no poisons of the physician are employed, this book is gratefully dedicated by -THE AUTHOR-" [Italics and all caps are vintage text.]

Considering my father's dedication to "natural hygiene," it's a great irony that he is best known as a snack food magnate. Dad's ideas about wholesome food seem diametrically opposed to the idea of snack food (which was once called "fun for you" food by Frito-Lay). However, my father's original concept for Fritos was to use simple, healthy ingredients. When Fritos were first introduced, they were advertised as a good, wholesome food, not just a snack. The following comes from an article called "Let's Start Cooking," published in the *Frito Bandwagon* at the beginning of the Cooking with Fritos campaign: "So, here's to good eatin', and we mean *good* eatin', for Fritos are a food . . . a *good* food, tasty, nourishing, full of corn rich pep and goodness!"

Although most people nowadays do not think of Fritos as a health food, I'm told that it's the favorite snack food of vegans. It still contains the same basic, healthy ingredients that were in its original recipe, including stone-ground corn. It's made up of a blend of yellow and white corn, and each chip is still, at least in the case of Fritos Originals, one-and-a-half inches long and seventy-thousandths of an inch thick.

The company is now aligning with my father's original intentions to sell high-quality, pure, natural, whole food. It is very interesting to me that this has come almost full circle, back to where it was when Dad was alive. (See chapter 11 for more on this.) ■

Dad and Uncle Earl with the adapted potato ricer they bought from Gustavo Olguin.

Recipes

Here are some vintage "health food" recipes.

Fritos Carrot Casserole (vintage)

❖ Add the carrots, onion, celery, seasonings, and corn chips to the milk and beaten egg. Mix together, pour into a greased casserole, and bake at 350 degrees for 30 minutes. Serves 6.

2   cups cooked carrots, cut into rings
⅓   cup finely chopped onion
¼   cup finely chopped celery
¾   teaspoon salt
⅛   teaspoon pepper
½   cup crushed Fritos corn chips,
1   cup milk
1   egg, beaten

I like the title of the next recipe. During the 1950s, giving things French names created the illusion that they were very elegant. I can picture a housewife with her apron on announcing to her family, "And here's the Fritos à la Champignons!"

1 cup fresh or 1 can (6 ounces)
   mushrooms, cut into pieces
1 cup grated American cheese
¾ cup chopped celery
1 cup lightly crushed Fritos
1 cup milk
½ teaspoon salt
1 egg, slightly beaten

Fritos à la Champignons (with mushrooms)
(vintage)

❖ Drain and chop the mushrooms. Add the remaining ingredients and mix together. Pour into a greased baking dish and bake at 350 degrees for 25 minutes. Serves 8.

The term "fluffs" in the next recipe is not related to Fritos brand pork rinds, which also went by that name. Nor are the Fritos "cheese" fluffs related to Cheetos.

1 teaspoon flour
1 cup milk
1 cup grated cheese
2 egg yolks, lightly beaten
   Dash salt
   Dash cayenne
2 egg whites, stiffly beaten
1 cup Fritos corn chips

Fritos Cheese Fluffs (vintage)

❖ Mix the flour and milk. Heat slowly until the mixture thickens. Add the grated cheese and lightly beaten yolks, salt, and cayenne. Fold into the stiffly beaten whites. Pour into a buttered casserole. Top with the corn chips. Bake at 250 degrees for 15–18 minutes. Serve at once. Serves 6–8.

4 eggs
1 twin-pack Fritos Green Onion
   Dip Mix
2 tablespoons milk
1 teaspoon Lawry's Seasoned
   Salt

Surprise Scrambled Eggs (vintage)

❖ To the eggs, add the twin pack of dip mix combined with the milk. Stir in the Lawry's Seasoned Salt and beat well. Cook slowly in butter until firm, stirring occasionally. Serves 2–3.

I can't warm up to this recipe, as hard as I try. But everyone has different tastes, so all I can say is try it.

3 tablespoons butter or
   margarine
¾ teaspoon salt
6 tablespoons flour
1 cup milk
4 eggs, cooked hard and
   chopped
¾ cup crushed Fritos corn chips,
1 egg, beaten

Egg Cutlets (vintage)

❖ Make a sauce of the butter or margarine, salt, flour, and milk. Add the chopped eggs and cool. Form into croquettes, dip into the beaten egg, roll in the Fritos corn chips and fry at 375 degrees. Serves 8.

My mother made the following recipe when we were kids in spite of the fact that she believed eggplant made her arthritis act up.

Fritos Eggplant Casserole (vintage)

❖ Combine the cubed eggplant with the onions, celery, and bell pepper. Steam until tender in a small amount of salted water. Mix the cheese, corn chips, and tomato sauce or soup ▶

and add ⅔ of this mixture to the steamed vegetables. Add the salt and pepper and mix well. Place in a glass baking dish. Top with the remaining ⅓ of the cheese mixture. Sprinkle more crushed corn chips on top and bake in a 350-degree oven until the cheese is well melted. Serve very hot. Yields 6–8 portions.

The next recipe is a little different than mine. I like to make barbecued lima beans because everyone can tell on sight they're not just canned food. The combination of flavors of barbecue sauce and limas is great in both versions—mine and Nell Morris's. Here is hers; I think you'll like it.

1 medium eggplant (about 1 pound), peeled and cut into ¼-inch cubes
2 medium onions, chopped
2 stalks celery, chopped
½ bell pepper, chopped
½ pound grated American cheese
½ bag (4 ounces) Fritos corn chips + more for topping
1 cup tomato sauce or condensed tomato soup
½ teaspoon salt
¼ teaspoon pepper

Fritos Barbecued Lima Beans (vintage)

❖ Sauté the onion in 1 tablespoon of the bacon fat. Add to the mashed butter beans. Then add the salt, grated cheese, and finely crushed corn chips. Mix together, form into balls, and roll in the coarsely crushed corn chips. Place in a baking pan that has been greased with the remaining tablespoon of fat. Pour the barbecue sauce over the balls and bake at 350 degrees for 30 minutes. Sprinkle crushed corn chips on top.

½ medium onion, chopped
1 + 1 tablespoons bacon fat (obviously a 1950s ingredient for which vegetable oil can substitute)
1½ cups cooked butter beans (limas), mashed
¼ teaspoon salt
½ cup grated American cheese,
¼ cup finely crushed Fritos corn chips
1 cup coarsely crushed Fritos corn chips + extra for a topping
1 recipe barbecue sauce (see recipe below)

Barbecue Sauce (vintage)

❖ Stir all ingredients for the sauce together.

I love the title of this recipe.

¾ cup ketchup
4 tablespoons vinegar
4 tablespoons brown sugar
2 tablespoons Worchestershire sauce
1 tablespoon mustard

Fritos Zippy Cheese Bake (vintage)

❖ Add the heated milk and the seasonings to the beaten eggs. Mix the onion, cheese, and corn chips together and pour into a greased 2-quart baking dish. Pour the milk and egg mixture over. Bake at 350 degrees for 20 minutes. Makes 6–8 servings.

1½ cups milk, heated
½ teaspoon dry mustard
1½ teaspoons salt
¼ teaspoon cayenne
2 eggs, slightly beaten
1 cup chopped onion
2 cups grated American cheese
1 cup crushed Fritos corn chips

I made a vegetarian version of this recipe—without the bacon and substituting vegetable oil for the bacon fat. It was very pretty and tasty.

½ medium size onion, chopped
4 ounces Fritos
4 ounces bread crumbs
½ milk
1 tablespoon butter
1 teaspoon flour

Fritos Squash
Serves Six

❖ Sauté chopped onions in small amount butter or margarine. Slice and steam squash in a small amount of water and season to taste. Spread layer of squash and chopped onion in casserole and cover with an equal mixture of bread crumbs and crushed Fritos. Repeat this procedure, making four layers. Make medium white sauce using ½ cup milk, 1 tablespoon butter and 1 tablespoon flour. Pour white sauce over sauce mixture and allow to penetrate. Cover top with layer of whole Fritos and bake in medium hot oven (350 degrees) for 20–30 minutes.

The addition of Fritos makes these scalloped potatoes, which are always good, even better.

4 cups peeled and thinly sliced Irish potatoes
¾ cup grated American cheese
Butter
Salt and paprika to taste
¾ cup crushed Fritos corn chips
1 cup or more of milk (or, for a deluxe dish, use slightly diluted cream of mushroom soup)

Scalloped Potatoes with Fritos (vintage)

❖ Cover the potatoes with cold water, let stand 15 minutes, and drain well. Arrange a layer in a greased baking dish, dot it with butter and season well with salt and paprika. Reserving ⅓ of the cheese, alternate layers of buttered, seasoned potatoes with grated cheese. Mix the remaining ⅓ cup of cheese with the crushed corn chips and add as the last layer. Pour the milk over all until it can be seen through the top layer. Bake at 350 degrees for 1¼ hours or until tender.

Sweet potatoes are more commonly served today as part of our rediscovery of natural flavors and regional foods. The recipe below reminds me of sweet potato fries, sweet potato chips, and other newly popular side dishes.

1½ cups mashed sweet potatoes
¼ teaspoon cinnamon
⅛ teaspoon nutmeg
2 tablespoons butter
Fritos corn chip crumbs

Fritos Sweet Potato Balls (vintage)

❖ Season the sweet potatoes and mash them together with the butter and seasoning. Form the mixture into balls and roll them in the corn chip crumbs. Bake at 350 degrees for 20 minutes.

Next I present the vintage Fritos recipes for salads and vegetables that I have collected.

Fritos à la Chef's Salad (vintage)

❖ Place the vegetables in a bowl. Make the dressing using the recipe below. While the dressing is still hot, pour it over the salad ingredients. Place the corn chips in a frying pan to which the olive oil has been added and heat. Stir until thoroughly hot and add to the salad. Garnish with lettuce and parsley. Makes 4–6 servings.

2	medium tomatoes, cut into large pieces
1	large white onion, diced
½	medium cucumber, diced
½	green pepper, chopped
¼	head lettuce, cut into large pieces, with some reserved for garnish
	Hot Dressing (see recipe below)
1	cup Fritos corn chips
1	tablespoon olive oil
1	sprig parsley for garnish

HOT DRESSING

❖ When the salad is ready to dress, heat the bacon drippings. Add the vinegar and seasonings to the drippings, and mix well.

2	tablespoons bacon drippings
2	tablespoons white vinegar
½	teaspoon salt
½	teaspoon paprika
⅛	teaspoon black pepper

The Towie brand olives referred to in the recipe below were another Frito-Lay product. They came under the Frito-Lay umbrella when the company acquired Belle Products, which it may have done because olives went into so many Fritos recipes, or maybe the olives were used in the recipes because the company had acquired Towie.

Southwestern Salad Meal (vintage)

❖ Sauté the beef and onion in a skillet with the salt. Add the drained beans and (if you so desire) hot sauce and heat. In a large salad bowl, layer the shredded lettuce, crumbled tortilla chips, beef and beans, most of the grated cheese, and the hot Tomato Dressing. Repeat. Garnish with the tomato wedges, ripe olives, the remaining cheese, and whole tortilla chips. Serves 6.

1	pound ground beef
1	can (15 ounces) kidney beans, drained
1	medium onion, chopped
½	teaspoon salt
	Hot sauce (if desired)
½	head lettuce, shredded
2	cups crumbled Nacho Cheese Flavored Doritos
1	cup grated American cheese, reserve some for garnish
	Tomato Dressing (recipe below)
2	medium tomatoes, cut into wedges
½	cup ripe olives (Towie or other)
	Whole Nacho Cheese Flavored Doritos for garnish

TOMATO DRESSING

❖ Mix the ingredients together and simmer for 10 minutes.

1	can (8 ounces) tomato sauce
½	medium onion, chopped fine
½	medium tomato, cut into small pieces
¼	teaspoon salt
½	teaspoon chili powder

Tostados Salad

1 head of lettuce, diced
4 tomatoes, cut into pieces
4 ounces grated Cheddar cheese
1 small onion, chopped
1 pound hamburger
  Dash hot sauce (or to taste)
1 can (15 ounces) kidney beans, drained
2 bags (7/8 ounce each) of Doritos, broken up in the bag
1 jar (8 ounces) thousand island dressing
1 avocado, sliced

❖ Mix together the lettuce, tomatoes, cheese, and onion. Brown the hamburger. Add the hot sauce and the beans and simmer for 10 minutes. Pour into the lettuce mixture. Dress with thousand island dressing. Toss and garnish with the broken Doritos and the sliced avocado.

Fritos Salad Mold (vintage)

1 package lime gelatin
1 cup orange juice, heated
1 teaspoon lemon juice
2 cups sliced pears and chopped canned pineapple (or use any seasonal fruit, or fruit cocktail)
  Melon balls
  Fritos corn chips

❖ Make lime gelatin according to the directions on the package, using the hot orange juice in place of hot water. Add the lemon juice and pour into a ring mold. Chill until the gelatin begins to set. Add the fruit, mix thoroughly, and continue to chill until firm. To serve: Turn the gelatin out of the mold. Fill the center of the salad with the melon balls and surround it with the corn chips. This salad is delicious served with a cream cheese dressing. Serves 6.

When I make a pear and cottage cheese salad with Fritos for lunch, I like the new canned pears that are packed in pear juice instead of sugar syrup. The pears taste almost as good as fresh and are so convenient for a quick lunch. I use a little Heinz salad cream in the hollow of the pear, and instead of serving the Fritos on the side I pour them on top of the salad.

Unlike Little Miss Muffet, my mother preferred her cottage cheese washed off in a colander so that the whey was removed from the curds. You may want to experiment with this for the next recipe if you don't normally like cottage cheese.

The following vintage recipe has the same basic ingredients I used in my pear and cottage cheese salad, although of course the original recipe used pears canned in heavy syrup and mayonnaise instead of salad cream.

Fritos Cling Peach and Cheese Salad (vintage)

1 pound cream-style cottage cheese
¼ teaspoon salt
2 tablespoons mayonnaise
1 cup lightly crushed Fritos corn chips
1 can (no. 2½) cling peach halves in heavy syrup, chilled
  Crisp lettuce for garnish

❖ Combine the cottage cheese with the salt, mayonnaise, and corn chips. Serve on the peach halves and garnish with lettuce. Makes 6 servings.

This version uses cream cheese instead of cottage cheese. The practice of slathering fruits with spreads disappeared in the 1950s.

Fritos Pears (vintage)

❖ Soften the cream cheese with milk. Mix in the crushed corn chips and spread on the pears. Garnish with the maraschino cherry and sprig of parsley.

1 package (3 ounces) cream cheese
  A little milk
⅓ cup Fritos corn chips, finely ground
1 can (no. 2 ½) cling pears halves in heavy syrup, chilled Maraschino cherry and parsley for garnish

I haven't made any of the next five congealed salads but have tasted some of them at family potlucks. I must admit the idea of the congealed tomato ring makes me quiver and not necessarily with delight.

Congealed Tomato Ring with Fritos Cheese (vintage)

❖ Soften the gelatin in cold water. Add to the hot tomato juice and stir until dissolved. Add the salt, horseradish, onion juice, and vinegar. Turn into a small ring mold that has been rinsed with cold water. Chill. Garnish with the corn chips and serve with Fritos Cheese.

1 envelope (1 tablespoon) unfla-vored gelatin
¼ cup cold water
2 cups tomato juice, heated
½ teaspoon salt
1 tablespoon prepared horseradish
1 tablespoon onion juice (strained from pureed onion if you can't find store-bought)
1 tablespoon mild vinegar
  Fritos Cheese (see recipe below)
  King-size Fritos corn chips for garnish

FRITOS CHEESE (vintage)

❖ Mix together the cream cheese and the milk. Add the corn chips and mix.

1 pakage (3 ounces) cream cheese
4 tablespoons milk
½ cup finely crushed Fritos corn chips

Congealed Cranberry Ring with Fritos Cheese (vintage)

❖ Dissolve the gelatin in the boiling water. Crush the cranberry sauce and add it to the hot gelatin. Pour half the gelatin mixture into a ring mold and chill until almost set. Place the pear slices in a ring on top of the gelatin. Add the remaining gelatin. When firm, turn the gelatin out of the mold and fill its center with Fritos Cheese (see the recipe above).

1 package (3 ounces) lemon flavored gelatin
1½ cups boiling water
1 cup jellied cranberry sauce
4 canned pear halves, sliced
  Fritos Cheese (see recipe above)

1 tablespoon gelatin
¼ cup cold water
1 egg yolk, slightly beaten
1 teaspoon salt
1 tablespoon sugar
1 teaspoon dry mustard
¼ cup vinegar
2 cups flaked salmon
½ cup celery, chopped
½ cup green peppers, chopped
½ cup heavy cream *or* thoroughly chilled evaporated milk, whipped
Fritos corn chips

Congealed Salmon Loaf (vintage)

❖ Soak the gelatin in cold water. Meanwhile mix the egg yolk with the salt, sugar, and mustard. Add the vinegar and cook over hot water until the mixture thickens. Remove from the fire and add the softened gelatin, stirring until dissolved. Add the salmon, celery, and peppers. Fold in the whipped cream. Pour into a mold and chill. Turn the salmon loaf out of the mold, and serve garnished with lots of corn chips.

The next recipe makes me think of family potlucks.

1 package (three ounces) lemon-flavored gelatin
1 cup boiling water
¾ cup cottage cheese, drained
¼ cup American cheese that has been cut into small cubes
1 can (9 ounces) crushed pineapple, drained (makes ¾ cup)
Fritos corn chips for garnish

Cheese and Pineapple in Lemon Gelatin Garnished with Fritos (vintage)

❖ Dissolve the gelatin in the boiling water. When cool add the cheeses and pineapple. Pour into a mold and chill until firm. Turn out of the mold, slice, and garnish with corn chips.

Helen L. Corbitt was the Director of Food Services for Neiman-Marcus from 1955 until sometime in the 1960s. She was an early advocate of using the finest, freshest ingredients. She was also the author of many cookbooks, among them Helen Corbitt's Cookbook, *which is one of the oldest cookbooks in my collection.*

When I was growing up in Dallas, our big treat for birthday celebrations was going to the Zodiac room at Neiman-Marcus for lunch. I always ordered the salad trio, which included Helen Corbitt's signature Orange Chiffon Gelatin, molded into individual servings.

1 tablespoon gelatin
¼ cup cold water
4 egg yolks, beaten until light
½ + ½ cup sugar, divided
½ teaspoon salt
1 tablespoon lemon juice
½ cup orange juice
1 tablespoon grated orange peel
4 egg whites

Orange Chiffon by Helen Corbitt (adapted)

❖ Soak the gelatin in the cold water for 15 minutes. Stir constantly while, to the beaten egg yolks, you add ½ cup of the sugar and the salt, lemon juice, and orange juice. Cook in a double boiler until thick. Add the grated orange peel. Remove from heat and add the gelatin. Stir until dissolved. Cool. Beat the egg whites medium-stiff, add the rest of the sugar gradually, and continue beating until stiff. Fold the egg whites into the gelatin and orange mixture. Then pour into individual molds and chill.

Greengage plums, used in the recipe below, seem like a 1950s phenomenon. Dr. Shelton did not recommend canned fruit and therefore I never tasted this recipe as a child.

Greengage Plum Salad Garnished with Fritos
(vintage)

❖ Dissolve the gelatin in the boiling water. Cool. When the mixture begins to thicken add the plums and grated cheese. Pour into molds and place in the refrigerator to congeal. Serve with mayonnaise and garnish with the corn chips.

1 package (3 ounces) lemon-flavored gelatin.
1 cup boiling water
1 cup canned greengage plums (sieved to remove stones), with their juice
1 cup grated American cheese Mayonnaise
1 cup Fritos corn chips

A friend in my writing group remembers that her mother made this dish for her when she was little.

Fritos Banana Logs (vintage)

❖ Peel the bananas and cut them in half crosswise. Roll in mayonnaise, then in crushed corn chips.

4 medium bananas
Mayonnaise
1 cup finely crushed Fritos

When I look at the recipe below all I can do is giggle and think, "Heaven help me."

Frito-Banana-Peanut Butter Salad (vintage)

❖ Peel the bananas and slice lengthwise. Mix together the peanut butter, mayonnaise, and jelly. Spread the mixture on the banana slices and sprinkle with Fritos. Server on lettuce.

4 medium bananas
4 tablespoons peanut butter
1 tablespoon mayonnaise
1 tablespoon grape jelly
½ cup crushed Fritos corn chips
Lettuce

This is another recipe for a dish straight off the family-reunion table.

Macaroni Salad (vintage)

❖ Combine all the ingredients except the corn chips and chill. Before serving, stir in the corn chips.

VARIATIONS
Add 1 cup shrimp, chicken, or other cold meat.

4 ounces elbow or fancy macaroni, cooked, drained, and cooled
¼ cup mayonnaise
2 tablespoons chopped onion
3 tablespoons chopped green pepper
3 tablespoons chopped dill pickle
¼ teaspoon salt
1 cup Swiss cheese cubes
1 cup lightly crushed Fritos corn chips

Chapter 10

Desserts

ALTHOUGH IN my family we almost never ate dessert or anything else with refined sugar in it, I was encouraged to learn to bake by my mother and my governess, Mrs. Verna Johnson. My first lesson as a dessert-maker was baking pineapple upside-down cake. Mrs. Johnson taught me how to make this simple but delicious cake with pineapple rings, maraschino cherries, brown sugar, butter, and a yellow cake mix.

Mrs. Johnson, as we always addressed her, on our porch, circa 1955. She did have a soft side, despite her stern appearance.

(This was the era when cake mixes were gaining popularity as a timesaving device for the busy housewife.)

The first recipe that I learned on my own was a Black Forest cake. I didn't pick it because it sounded good—I picked it because it was the longest recipe in my *Joy of Cooking* cookbook. Like my father, I was an experimental cook who made things over and over until I got them right, even perfect—that was how I learned to follow a recipe and how I learned to make Black Forest cake. The layers of the cake had to be split in half using a thread and toothpicks. I discovered that you had to weave the thread alternately under and over the toothpicks before pulling the thread to tighten the circle; I tried several times before I finally got the hang of it. The whole thing was not just a lesson in following a recipe, but in reading a diagram (and then improvising to make it work).

My next challenge was divinity, a light, extremely sweet candy made with egg whites; I chose it because my mother told me it was one of the most difficult candies to make. She knew this from her food preparation classes in college. Again, I made divinity several times before perfecting it. Maybe I was trying to impress my mother, since she had said how hard it was.

Interestingly, I have found a number of recipes in our family archives that use Fritos as an ingredient in desserts. Although it is hard to believe that a Frito dessert can work, I have tried some of the recipes, such as Fritos Chocolate Crunchies and Mincemeat Whip, and I find them to be quite good. After all, Mother Doolin's fruitcake was the original recipe that incorporated Fritos and kicked off the Cooking with Fritos campaign. Other Fritos dessert recipes, such as Fritos Molasses Pie and Fritos Yum-Yums (dates blended with peanut butter and rolled in crushed Fritos), leave something to be desired.

Because my family rarely ate desserts, I had never tried most of these recipes until recently. I do remember that my mother made us a rhubarb pie once. I don't remember exactly what she did (she probably substituted honey for sugar), but I do know that she murdered the recipe—I hated the result and never wanted to eat rhubarb pie again. I have to admit that my mother wasn't a very good cook overall. This might have been at least partly explained by the fact that Mom had virtually no sense of smell, and this affected her ability to taste things the way she was supposed to. I believe she could have had surgery

AMERICA'S FAVORITE—Make menus
sparkle with FRITOS, golden chips of sun-
ripened corn. In favorite recipes, with beverages, soups, salads—FRITOS are always
delicious. Enjoy crisp, flavor-rich FRITOS,
first choice of millions!

FRITOS is the registered trade mark of The Frito Co.

*Fritos Molasses Pie and Fritos
Chocolate Squares pictured on the
back of a recipe booklet printed
sometime in the 1940s*

to correct the problem, but that would have been against her beliefs and Dr. Shelton's teachings.

I recently made a rhubarb pie for my son using a combination of commercially grown rhubarb and some that grows wild in my yard in Colorado. My son gave it one taste and his reaction was like the one I had as a child. But I loved this pie. Unlike the pie my mother made, it was sweet, and it contained aromatic cardamom and freshly ground nutmeg. I don't think those fresh gourmet spices were even available in Dallas back when my mother baked her rhubarb pie. The fresh cardamom and nutmeg made all the difference.

Recently I made the vintage recipe for Fritos Molasses Pie. The recipe was first published in the *Frito Bandwagon* in 1952. I mixed up the ingredients for the filling and poured them into a shell made of crushed corn chips and other dry ingredients, then sprinkled some crushed Fritos on top (after I had cooked the pie a little to make the filling firm enough to keep the Fritos from sinking to the bottom). When the pie came out of the oven, it looked like something made out of motor oil sludge (it should have been named "Petroleum Pie") and I can only describe the taste as borderline awful.

The recipe for this pie was based on an even older recipe that was probably created during the Depression. After I baked the pie, my husband Alan and I sat down at the kitchen table and tasted it. We made eye-popping, lip-smacking faces at each other, joking that this Depression-era pie *was* depressing, as we emptied the rest of it into the trash. (See the recipes at the end of chapter 12, "Cooking with Fritos Today," for some ways I adapted this recipe to make it more palatable.) ■

Recipes

Fritos Molasses Pie (vintage)

This pie shell is delicious in many different recipes.

⅓ cup shortening
1 cup flour
¾ teaspoon salt
1 teaspoon baking powder
1 cup crushed Fritos corn chips
 Ice water

3 eggs
1⅓ cups molasses (unsulfured)
½ teaspoon nutmeg
½ teaspoon cinnamon
½ teaspoon salt
2 tablespoons melted butter or margarine
½ cup brown sugar
1 tablespoon cornstarch
½ cup crushed Fritos corn chips

FRITOS PIE SHELL
❖ Cut the shortening with the flour, salt, and baking powder. Add the corn chips and enough ice water to hold the dough together. Roll out onto a floured board. Line the pan with the dough and prick with a fork.

PIE FILLING
❖ Beat the eggs and to them add the molasses, nutmeg, cinnamon, salt, and melted butter or margarine. Combine the brown sugar and cornstarch and add to the molasses mixture. Pour into the unbaked pie shell and bake at 400 degrees long enough to firm the filling a little. Then sprinkle the top of the pie with the corn chips. Bake at 400 degrees for 15 minutes, then reduce the heat to 350 degrees and bake for another 30 minutes.

Many of these desserts sound antiquated and even unappealing. For example, one of my friends has a hard time believing that Fritos mix well with fudge. But if you think about it, chocolatiers have been mixing crunchy and sometimes salty ingredients into chocolate for years—take, for example, Nestlé's Crunch bars or chocolate-covered pretzels.

2 cups sugar
3 tablespoons cocoa
¾ cup sweet milk
3 tablespoons butter
½ teaspoon vanilla
1 cup crushed Fritos corn chips

Fritos Fudge (vintage)

❖ Thoroughly mix the sugar and cocoa in a saucepan. Add the milk, stirring it in, and set over a good-sized heavy saucepan set on high heat. Stir constantly until the fudge comes to a boil. Allow it to boil slowly until it strings or until it forms a soft ball in a cup of water. Remove it from the stove, add the butter and vanilla, and beat until almost thick enough to pour. Then add the crushed corn chips and pour into a buttered pan.

Fritos Baked Apples (vintage)

❖ Core the apples and place them in a 9-inch relatively deep pie pan or a 2.6-quart casserole. Mix the sugar and cinnamon. Fill each apple with one tablespoon of the sugar mixture, two dates, two marshmallows, and two pecan halves. Top with the corn chips. Pour the cup of water around the apples and bake at 350 degrees for 50 minutes or until tender. Serve with whipped cream.

6	large baking apples
6	tablespoons sugar
¾	teaspoon cinnamon
12	dates
12	marshmallows
12	pecan halves
½	cup Fritos corn chips
1	cup water
½	cup whipping cream, whipped

I made homemade cookies for a guest who was visiting from France and staying in our home. She loved the wonderful sweet smells in the kitchen and said that in France they always buy cookies from the bakery or the store—they never make them at home. The cookie recipes below are really good—when baked into a cookie, Fritos become nutty-tasting and the scent of the baking Fritos is mouth-watering.

Fritos Chocolate Cookies (vintage)

❖ Melt the butter or margarine and chocolate in a double boiler. Add the sugar, egg, flour, salt, and vanilla. Pour into a greased 6½x10½-inch pan. Sprinkle with the corn chips. Bake at 400 degrees for 12 minutes. Cut into squares. Makes 24 cookies.

⅓	cup butter or margarine
1	square semi-sweet chocolate
½	cup sugar
1	egg
¼	cup flour
⅛	teaspoon salt
1	teaspoon vanilla
½	cup crushed Fritos corn chips

Nell Morris was both a dietician and a chef. In 1951 she was the president of the Texas Dietetic Association. The cookies below were originally named Fritos Chocolate Crunchies, but Nell Morris renamed them Texdias in honor of the Texas Dietetic Association. I also found the same recipe in an old pamphlet in Frito Lay's new kitchen library at the Plano headquarters; that version of the recipe was called Fritos Chocolate Jets and was probably written by Mary Livingston, Dad's executive secretary. The fact that the pamphlet containing the original recipe was printed during Mary Livingston's involvement in testing recipes at the office means that this is one of the oldest Fritos recipes and was created right at the beginning of the Cooking with Fritos concept.

I found an undated old ad that says, about these cookies, "For munching after the game and at TV-time, Fritos Chocolate Crunchies are wonderful! Simply add crushed Fritos to melted chocolate, drop by spoonfuls on waxed paper, chill and serve."

This recipe for cookies is my favorite vintage Frito recipe; it was also the first one I made, or tried to make. (See chapter 11 for more vintage recipes.) I sometimes make a variation using the new "Flamin' Hot" Fritos instead of the originals, and I ▶

▶▶ also put in a cup of roasted pumpkin seeds. I call this "Kaleta's Frito Pepita Diablo." Another variation is to add peppermint oil to the original recipe (if you're using regular peppermint oil, add a quarter teaspoon, but some new peppermint oils are steam-extracted and have much higher potency, so at most you'd want to use only a drop). This variation of the recipe is called "Fritos Chocolate Mint Crunchies."

---

1 package (6 ounces) semi-sweet chocolate
1½ cups lightly crushed Fritos corn chips

Fritos Chocolate Crunchies (vintage)

❖ Melt the chocolate over hot water. Add the crushed Fritos and drop by spoonfuls on wax paper. Chill and serve. Makes two dozen cookies.

---

1 bar Baker's Bittersweet Chocolate
½ can sweetened condensed milk
1 cup crushed Fritos corn chips

Fritos Chocolate Squares (vintage)

❖ Melt the chocolate over hot water. Add the milk and mix. Stir in the crushed Fritos. Pour into a buttered pan and cut into squares. Makes 16 squares.

The next recipe (along with some of the others in this section) may sound like it was made up just to sell Fritos, but it's actually quite good (though I make no claims for its nutritional value).

---

1 package fudge mix (follow package directions for frosting)
¾ cup crushed Fritos corn chips

Fritos Party Fudge Frosting (vintage)

❖ When you have made the frosting, add the ¾ cup corn chips. Use at once.

---

1 teaspoon salt
3 cups boiling water
½ cup regular, old-fashioned grits
½ cup milk
1 beaten egg
   Maple syrup
   Vegetable, canola, or corn oil for frying

Fritos Squares with Maple Syrup (vintage)

❖ Add the salt to the water and bring to a boil. Pour the grits slowly and steadily into the boiling water. Cook for 15 minutes, then spread into a square cake pan. When cold, cut into squares. Combine the milk and beaten egg. Dip the squares into this mixture, then into the corn chips. Fry in ½ inch of oil until brown. Serve with maple syrup. Serves 6.

1¾ cups flour
2 tablespoons sugar
½ teaspoon salt
4 teaspoons baking powder
2 eggs, separated
1¼ cups milk ▶

Fritos Pecan Waffles (vintage)

❖ Measure and sift together the flour, sugar, salt, and baking powder. Beat the egg yolks and add the milk, mixing thoroughly. Pour the milk mixture into the flour mixture gradually and stir until smooth. Stir in the melted shortening, slightly cooled. ▶

▶▶ Beat the egg whites until stiff and fold them in. Add the pecans and corn chips last. (Leftover batter, if covered, can be stored in the refrigerator.) Serves 6.

▶▶ 6 tablespoons melted short-ening
½ cup chopped pecans
½ cup crushed Fritos corn chips
Pam spray for the griddle

Sweet potato pie is a southern soul food tradition. The only thing better than sweet potato pie is Fritos Sweet Potato Pie.

Fritos Sweet Potato Pie (vintage)

❖ Mix the mashed sweet potatoes and the milk, sugar, eggs, and seasonings. Pour into an unbaked pie shell and top with the crushed corn chips. Bake at 450 degrees for 10 minutes. Then re-duce the heat to 325 degrees and bake for another 35 minutes.

1½ cups sweet potatoes, mashed
1 cup milk
½ cup sugar
2 eggs
1 teaspoon salt
1 teaspoon cinnamon
½ cup crushed Fritos corn chips

Since my dad originally sold ice cream along with the other treats at the Doolin family's Highland Park Confectionery, he may have influenced Fritos' marketing department to distribute the following "Fritos with ice cream" dessert recipes, especially in the summertime.

Fritos Chocachip Ice Cream (vintage)

❖ Melt the chocolate and stir in the corn chips. Pour onto waxed paper and spread rather thinly Chill and break into small pieces. Add to your favorite homemade ice cream mix just before the ice cream hardens, or follow this recipe for a good, custard ice cream.

4 ounces semi-sweet chocolate
¾ cup finely crushed Fritos corn chips
Homemade ice cream (your favorite, or using the recipe below)

Ice Cream Custard

❖ Heat the 2 cups of milk. Mix the flour and water to form a paste, then add the hot milk, stir like mad and cook until thickened. Add the sugar, salt, and slightly beaten egg yolks, cook for 30–45 minutes, remove from the heat, and allow to thoroughly cool. Whip the chilled evaporated milk thoroughly and fold it into the cooled custard. Add the vanilla and pour the mixture into a freezing tray. When the ice cream is partially frozen add the chocolate chips you have made, then freeze until firm.

2 cups milk
2 tablespoons flour
2 tablespoons water
⅔ cup sugar
¼ teaspoon salt
2 egg yolks, lightly beaten
1 cup chilled evaporated milk, whipped
1 teaspoon vanilla

Fritos Ice Cream Pie with Strawberries (vintage)

❖ Fill the pastry shell with the ice cream and cover the top with the finely crushed corn chips. Place whole fresh strawberries around the top, saving several for the center.

Precooked pastry shell
1 pint vanilla ice cream
Finely crushed Fritos corn chips
Whole strawberries

1 can sweetened condensed milk
½ cup lemon juice
Green, yellow, and pink food coloring
1 Fritos pie shell (see recipe above under "Fritos Molasses Pie")
Whipped cream

Fritos Rainbow Pie (vintage)

❖ Mix the milk and lemon juice. Divide into three portions, coloring one green, one yellow, and one pink. Spread in layers in the Fritos pie shell. Chill and top with whipped cream.

Frito Lay recently asked me to be the first on-camera judge for a new Web site called "Fritos Pie Remix" they've started that reintroduces the idea of cooking with Fritos. While I was being filmed for the Web site and for YouTube, I taste-tested a "Fluffernutter" Pie made with a crust of crumbled chocolate cookies and food-processed Fritos. (While I write this the video is still being edited and isn't available yet on the Internet.) The crust's outer ring was a dark-colored chocolate cookie crumb and the center was a circle of golden Fritos. The two colors made a pretty contrast in the pie pan. The filling was made of a mixture that was marshmallow and peanut-butter flavored. I was expecting the pie to be good and I wasn't disappointed. The saltiness of the Fritos made it taste a little like a Reese's peanut butter cup.

1 envelope unflavored gelatin
½ + ½ cup cold water
3 tablespoons sugar
1 teaspoon vanilla extract
1 cup peanut butter
1 cup Marshmallow Fluff
2 cups heavy or whipping cream
1 Fritos Chocolate Crumb Crust (see recipe below)

Fluffernutter Pie
By Steven Kalil

❖ In a medium saucepan combine the gelatin and ½ cup of the cold water; let stand 1 minute. Add the sugar and cook, stirring constantly, until the gelatin is completely dissolved. Remove from heat. Stir in the vanilla and remaining water. Beat in the peanut butter and Marshmallow Fluff. Chill until the mixture mounds when dropped from spoon. Whip the cream into soft peaks and fold into the Fluffernutter mix. Turn into the crust: chill until set. Makes 6–8 servings.

10 chocolate wafer cookies
2 cups crushed Fritos corn chips
6 tablespoons butter or margarine, melted

FRITOS CHOCOLATE CRUMB CRUST

❖ Crush the cookies into fine crumbs and combine with the melted butter. Pour into an 8- or 9- or 10-inch pie plate.

4 tablespoons butter or margarine
16 marshmallows
1¾ cups finely crushed Fritos corn chips

Fritos Pie Crust for Ice Cream (vintage)

❖ Melt the butter and dissolve the marshmallows in it. Add the corn chips and stir. Pour into a pie pan and press into shape. Fill the crust with ice cream. (Or, you can simply pour chocolate or other flavorings over ice cream and sprinkle crushed corn chips atop it. Nell Morris wrote, "You'll be amazed and pleased at the extra goodness those crunchy corn chips add. Or if you don't have flavorings available, just top your ice cream with crushed corn chips; it's really a delightful surprise.")

With Dad's predilection for dates, I suspect the Fritos Yum-Yum recipe was created at his suggestion. These are sometimes called "Date Nut Perfections" in the old Frito literature. The next is my recipe for a contemporary version that is more fruity.

Fritos Yum-Yums (vintage)

❖ Cut the dates into fine pieces. Blend with the peanut butter. Form into balls the size of a walnut. Roll in the crushed corn chips and serve.

¾ cup pitted dates
3   tablespoons peanut butter
⅓ cup finely crushed Fritos corn chips

Fruity Fritos Yum Yums (contemporary)

❖ In a food processor, mix the first six ingredients until they form a ball. Toast the pecan pieces on a cookie sheet under broiler. Place the processed mixture and the pecans in a bowl. Add the minced apricots, the lemon zest and juice, and the contents of the processor. Knead it all together. Roll into 36 bite-sized balls. Roast the sesame seeds in a skillet until brown. Pour into a separate bowl and roll half of the bite-sized balls in the coconut. Roll the other half of the bite-sized balls in the sesame. Yields about 72 one-bite pieces.

1   cup Fritos corn chips
¾ cup pitted dates
¾ cup Calimyrna figs, stems removed
3   tablespoons smooth organic unsalted peanut butter
1   teaspoon fresh lemon juice
¼ cup amber Agave nectar
¾ cup pecan pieces
⅓ cup minced dried apricots
1   small lemon, zested and squeezed
½ cup organic unsweetened coconut (Let's Go Organic brand), finely shredded for baking
½ cup raw hulled sesame seeds

At one family brunch, I told my family that I planned to make the Frito dessert recipe for Mincemeat Whip. Everyone laughed. I imagine that the mental image everyone had was of hamburger meat in a blender. But "meat" here refers to the meat of apples and raisins (although in the past "mincemeat" did include meat as a traditional ingredient). Despite my family's reaction, this recipe is actually pretty good. The idea for making a whip that incorporates fruit may have been influenced by European cuisine. This recipe could have been named "Pippin Apple/Raisin Soufflé with Fritos" and sounded more appealing.

I took this dish for employees to taste-test at our not-for-profit editing studio for documentary films. Soufflé does not travel well, but I figured that the taste would be the same. Responses were, "Very delicate," "An unexpected combination of textures and flavors," "The Fritos become nutty and crunchy—very flavorful."

3   egg whites
¼   cup sugar
¾   cup mincemeat
½   cup crushed Fritos corn chips

Mincemeat Whip (vintage)

❖ Beat the egg whites until stiff, adding sugar gradually. (I learned while I was making this recipe that cold eggs are hard to separate and a broken yolk is more likely. Let eggs warm to room temperature for easy separation.) Fold in the mincemeat. Pour into a buttered baking dish and sprinkle with the corn chips. Pour into a soufflé pan (or 8 individual buttered custard cups) and set that pan (or the custard cups) in a larger pan of hot water. Bake one hour at 350 degrees in a pan of water. Serves 6.

Chapter 11

Then and Now

RECENTLY met Indra Nooyi for the first time. She is the current CEO of PepsiCo. (Frito Lay merged with PepsiCo in 1965.) PepsiCo is a conglomerate made up of Pepsi, Frito Lay, Tropicana, Quaker, and Gatorade. Having read about Indra in the cover story of the March 2008 issue of *Fortune* magazine, I felt as if I knew her already. I was impressed by the similarities between her and my dad. In bold font, the magazine says, "As a vegetarian, she's not who you'd think would be leading the maker of sugary soda and salty snacks." This is a perfect parallel to Dad, the vegetarian, health-obsessed leader of the early snack food industry. Indra has led PepsiCo in a more healthful and environmentally friendly direction since she joined it in 1994. PepsiCo's previous CEO, Roger Enrico, had also started turning the company in that direction, acquiring companies that made healthful beverages such as Aquafina, Tropicana, and Sobe. He also acquired Quaker Oats in 2001 and announced in 2002 the removal of trans fats from Doritos, Tostitos, and Cheetos.

Naked Juice is the company's newest acquisition, following Izze sparkling soda, Lipton bottled iced tea (this is a joint venture of PepsiCo with Lipton), Starbucks canned Frappuccino (a joint venture with Starbucks), Miss Vickie's chips, Flat Earth fruit and veggie chips, and True North products. Both Roger Enrico and now Indra Nooyi's initiatives are a move from "fun for you" to "better for you" and "good for you" products, to use the company's successive marketing language.

I believe this is a direction Dad wanted to take the company in right from the start. My father's knowledge about food, from growing to consuming, was vast. Dad's experimental sesame crops in Midlothian and Big Wells were a step in the direction of the health food market. I suspect he was considering using sesame oil as a secret ingredient in his vegetable oil blend, but

I don't know for sure because the oil blend was and still is a secret. As the president of the Frito Company, in 1936 Dad became the first person to import sesame oil from Japan, and his involvement in developing, selling, and finding new uses for cold-rolled sesame oil was extensive.

In addition to producing sunflower oil and cold-rolled sesame oil, Dad considered producing sesame candy. He found a cheap source of dried date crumbles and soon developed a recipe using sesame and dates (see the recipe section of this chapter). Both sesame candy and cold-rolled sesame oil are standards in health-food grocery stores today. The antioxidant properties of sesame seeds give foods made with them greater freshness and a longer shelf life. The oil of sesame seeds stays fresh for years.

Dad was interested in forward-looking agricultural practices that might be considered "green" farming today. In a letter to his father-in-law he suggested an experiment using manure from the cattle pens as a compost to grow alfalfa. He also wanted

Dad (in his Bogart suit) giving instructions to John Campbell, among blooming sesame plants. Dad's venture into sesame was a step in the direction of the health food market.

to study root rot as it affected alfalfa and how to overcome it. He hoped that he and Grandpa Coleman could solve the problem on their own, but he wanted to make investigations through the authorities as well, so he got involved with the Southwest Agricultural Institute. In late May of 1959, only a couple of months before his death, Dad was appointed a trustee of the Institute.

My father died at the age of 56. He had a number of heart attacks over a period of years and the last one killed him. Helen Harden, who was still working at the company when my father died, said, "In 1952 Mr. Doolin had already had a couple of heart attacks. In 1954 Mr. Doolin had a severe heart attack and that was the time when he brought in John Williamson to be the executive vice president. He had a couple more and then [had another] the year when he died. That was 1959."

After his initial heart attacks Dad knew he might not make it, and he prepared the company to proceed without him by appointing a capable president and vice president. He retired and became the chairman of the Frito Company board on June 10, 1959, a month before he died. I believe Dad might have been prepared for his death, but it came as a big shock to us. My brothers and my sister and I were staying with my grandfather at the Rio Vista because Dad was sick, but we had no idea how sick he was. We didn't get to say good-bye.

I never imagined that my father could die. Apparently, neither did most people at the Frito Company. According to Helen Harden, "It was a tremendous shock [to the whole company] when he passed away. We all knew that he had had some heart problems, but we thought that he was going to continue. But this time he didn't come back."

I remember the caravan of cars going to Dad's funeral from San Antonio to Dallas as an endless line of vehicles, all with their headlights on to signify our mourning. I was very impressed that so many people were affected by our loss. It all seemed unreal to me. I really loved him and missed him.

Mom was devastated by his death. She had worshiped him, and was left alone to finish raising us kids. When my father died, my brother Charles was thirteen, my brother Earl was twelve, I was nine, my sister Willa was six, and my youngest brother, Danny, was nine months old. My mother was still young and beautiful at forty. Her attempts at two subsequent marriages failed, probably because she was still in love with Dad.

Dad in the board room, flanked by
the new company president and vice-
president. Dad was signing over the
presidency to become the Chairman
of the board. He died a month later.

The men Dad had appointed to be president and vice president of the company were John D. Williamson and Fladger Tannery. They, along with many other loyal employees, including Lamar Lovvorn, who by that time was secretary and controller, kept the company going during the transition and beyond and hammered out the merger with Herman Lay in 1961. This merger was a strategy to expand the company to the Eastern seaboard.

Dad had been working on the merger before his death, but he'd had problems with the Lay company's profit margins and its failure to diversify—Dad felt Lay was not producing enough corn chips and that the possibility of potato-crop failure put the Lay Company at too much risk. Dad knew that the potato fungus that caused the famous Irish potato famine in the 1840s had migrated from Mexico to the United States at that time, and he felt that using potatoes as the sole crop to power an entire business was risky. Lay eventually saw the wisdom of Dad's advice to diversify into corn chips as well. Lay asked for help in diversifying and the merger was eventually accomplished. Later—in 1965—Frito-Lay merged with PepsiCo.

The year after my father died, the *Frito Bandwagon* acquired a new subtitle: "The New Era." The magazine also moved to a larger format. Eventually, Herman Lay became president of the company. I've been told that Herman Lay's management style was very different from Dad's. According to Helen Harden, "Mr. Doolin told you his dreams and how we could move forward. Mr. Lay said, 'This is how it's going to be.'"

In the world at large, the era in which Dad helped found and grow the Frito Company I think of as the "every-man-for-himself" era. The race for patents during that time is fascinating. How did Dad have so much knowledge and foresight? I wonder about him and Walt Disney and J. Bard Rousseau (who according to Mom was one of the inventors of the iron lung) and what makes people like them succeed.

This could be the recipe for their success: Take one part ambition, add knowledge and a pinch of passion, and finish with skill.

I read a quote from Arnold D. Glasgow that seems to fit Dad's modus operandi. According to Glasgow, "Success isn't a result of spontaneous combustion. You must set yourself on fire."

Dad, Disney, and Rousseau were all inventors in the same era. After my father's death, I became obsessed with the hope that since Disney was frozen cryogenically, maybe my father

Dad and Walt Disney with the mechanical, talking Frito Kid at the Casa de Fritos. Mr. Disney, or "Uncle Walt" as he told my siblings and me to call him, is plugging in a nickel here to bring the talking Frito Kid to life—and send a bag of Fritos sliding down the chute.

had also been frozen. My train of thought went like this: Disney was frozen; Dad and Disney were inventor friends, as were Dad and Rousseau (who could have invented other, possibly cryogenics-related medical equipment as well as his version of the iron lung); all three were ahead of their times; maybe Dad and Disney talked about the future; maybe Dad came to believe in cryogenics; maybe Mother kept it a secret; and maybe I would be able to see my father alive again.

I used to have a recurring dream that I saw someone on a crowded sidewalk who looked like Dad from behind; the man turned around and it was Dad, and after that he came back to live with us. When I woke up I always felt disoriented, because the dream seemed so real. ■

Recipes

I unearthed some of my dad's handwritten cooking-experiment notes from 1957. He was looking for recipes that could be served at Casa de Fritos in Disneyland. The following is his recipe for sesame candy with date crumbles. His notes about this cooking experiment are two pages long. In them he notes that date crumbles "can be run through a machine like a Waring blender and made into a paste or date butter." I am reminded of my sister Willa's current favorite snack, a 90-percent raw Larabar, which has a sticky date paste as a binder. I think that Dad's experiment was inspired by his health food interest. Date as a base for fruit and nut bars is very popular now, so once again Dad was before his time.

Dad's Experimental Sesame-Date Pralines

(vintage)

1½ cups light brown sugar
1½ cups milk
½ cup toasted sesame seeds
1 cup date butter

❖ Put the sugar and milk into a deep pot over high heat. Test the mixture as it cooks. Just before it reaches the soft-ball stage (a small amount dropped in cold water forms a soft ball), add the sesame seeds. Remove from the stove and beat in the date butter with a wooden spoon until smooth. Drop by spoonfuls on waxed paper. Let cool overnight. The texture is chewy and the flavor is delicious.

Back in the 1950s, Mom and Dad anticipated many of today's food trends. We were raised on goat's milk and fruits, nuts, and vegetables. Mom bought fresh goat milk as well as Norwegian Gjetost cheese (a mixture of cow's and goat's milk). Today we have wonderful local soft goat cheeses as well as a huge variety of goat cheeses from around the world. The Chavrie Company has begun to suggest new ways to use its products, attaching recipes to its packaging, and suggesting soft goat cheese as a dip ingredient instead of sour cream or cream cheese. I think of goat cheese as the new sour cream and cream cheese. Frank X. Tolbert Jr.—X ^{2}, as he calls himself— the son of Frank X. Tolbert Sr., creator of the famous "bowl of red" chili, told me he recommends putting grated hard goat cheese and chopped red onions on top in his version of Fritos Pie (see chapter 8, "Fritos Chili Pie," for his recipe).

The dawn of my experiments in cooking with Fritos—combining vintage Fritos recipes and adapting and updating them— occurred accidentally when my Fritos Chocolate Crunchies didn't harden in time for a party. My guests had already arrived, so I put the aborted cookies in the freezer; I put the melted chocolate into the middle of my chip-and-dip tray and surrounded it with Fritos, thus inventing Fritos Chocolate Fondue. Later I substituted Fritos Scoops for regular Fritos and found them more suitable for dipping. I discovered that freezing the Chocolate Crunchies hardened the chocolate and made the cookies even better.

Fritos Chocolate Fondue (original)

By Kaleta Doolin

4   dark chocolate bars (3 ½ ounces each)
Fritos Scoops corn chips

❖ Melt the chocolate in a double boiler. Place the chocolate in the center of a tray surrounded by the corn chips.

In all my travels and all the restaurants I've visited, I've found many ingredients that I now regularly use to update vintage recipes with the complex flavors of today. (Photo by Pat Haverfield, Haverfield Studios)

Chapter 12

Cooking with Fritos Today

LOVE to update classic recipes. I have been tasting lots of Southwestern foods and developing my own recipes as well as variations on some of the vintage Fritos recipes included in this book. My thinking about cooking has evolved in recent years. And my repertoire of ingredients has grown to include a range of different types of ground peppers for making chili along with seasoned rubs for venison and quail. I've also begun using new types of presentations, such as coulis—liquefied preparations drizzled or dotted onto the plate to provide a separate, small taste, tiny sample, or subtle flavor change or combination of flavors. I found out the hard way that old-fashioned decorating tools like pastry bags and cake-decorators with shaped nozzles—the kind that make stars, leaves, petals, and so forth—create old-fashioned-looking results and are therefore not the best choice for making updated-looking plates. These days all you need is a squirt bottle or a decorator with one round nozzle.

Here are some miscellaneous ingredients that I have found useful for updating dishes to create new versions for the palate of today: Ancho chili powder, arugula, black sesame seeds, cardamom, curry, fresh fennel, flat-leaf parsley, Hatch (Anaheim) green chilies, Meyer lemons, Agave nectar, orange zest, quinoa, and flake finishing salt.

In addition, I've begun using a food processor to make Fritos into an oily masa (masa is the original ingredient from which Fritos are made). The masa made from Fritos has great potential as an ingredient in tamales and other recipes. I recently served a layered salad that had mangoes and avocados, and, on the side, Fritos, to a curator from the Mid-America Arts Alliance. After lunch she commented, "It's surprising how well the salad goes with the crunch and flavor of Fritos." (See below for

Chef Jennifer McKinney and I had a blast creating this Margarita, Mango Salsa and Avocado Congealed Salad. The family tradition goes on. (Photo by Pat Haverfield, Haverfield Studios)

the recipe, called Margarita, Mango Salsa, and Avocado Congealed Salad.)

I've found that Fritos are an amazingly adaptable ingredient. Their crunchy texture and salty corn taste make a great counterpoint to sweet ingredients, and their familiar flavor adds a little taste of nostalgia to many contemporary gourmet recipes. Along with the results of my own Frito-cooking experiments, I've included below some recipes by contemporary chefs who also have featured Fritos as an ingredient. ■

Recipes

I love salads with pears and avocado. My train of thought took me to many Texas-related possibilities before I arrived at the recipe below for Margarita, Mango Salsa, and Avocado Congealed Salad. I looked at several vintage recipes that used gelatin and Fritos, or gelatin with Fritos on the side, including Fritos Pears, Congealed Tomato Ring with Fritos Cheese, and Congealed Cranberry Ring with Fritos Cheese, all presented in chapter 9, "Natural Hygiene," and, Fritos Salad Mold, in chapter 2, "Cooking with Fritos." I tried making gelatin with lime juice, pears, and avocado, but the lime juice overpowered the other flavors and the whole thing said Florida instead of Texas to me. With the help of personal chef Jennifer McKinney, I decided to use mangoes instead of pears to add a bit of punch and a touch of Mexico.

Margarita, Mango Salsa, and Avocado Congealed Salad

By Kaleta Doolin and Chef Jennifer McKinney

½ cup water + ¼ cup cold water
½ cup + ¼ cup Bacardi frozen, concentrated margarita mix
2 envelopes unflavored gelatin
1 cup water, heated + ¼ cup cold water

FIRST PREPARE THE GELATIN MIXTURE:

❖ Heat the water with the ½ cup of frozen margarita mix. Next, in a separate bowl, mix ¼ cup *cold* water with the ¼ cup of margarita mix. Sprinkle the two envelopes of gelatin into the cold mixture and let sit for 5 minutes. Whisk the cold mixture into the hot mixture until all the gelatin is dissolved.

NEXT, MAKE THE MANGO SALSA:

¾ cup mango (1 mango, seeded and cut into ¼-inch dice)
¼ cup minced jalapeños
4 teaspoons lime juice
1 teaspoon orange juice
½ tablespoon honey
⅛ teaspoon salt

❖ Mix all the salsa ingredients together.

NOW MAKE THE MOLDED PART OF THE SALAD:

3 avocados (slightly underripe so that they don't have any unsightly brown spots)
Meyer lemon juice
1/16 teaspoon garlic powder
1/16 teaspoon salt
1/16 teaspon cumin powder, mixed together ▶

❖ Spray a 9-inch ring mold (or, you can use an or 8½x4x3-inch silicone loaf pan) with Pam. Pour the salsa into the empty mold and distribute evenly over the bottom. Pour in some of the hot gelatin mixture to cover, and shake to be sure that it completely encases the mango salsa. Leave the rest of the gelatin mixture out of the refrigerator so that it doesn't congeal or melt it back down if it does. Chill until almost set. Slice the avocados into ½-inch slices and dip them in lemon juice to prevent browning. Arrange the sliced avocados in a ring over the mango salsa layer. Mix seasonings together and sprinkle the seasonings you mixed together over the avocados. Top the mold with the rest of the gelatin mix. Chill until firm. To unmold, carefully place in a hot bath (not letting the water rise higher than the sides of the mold) until you can see a little liquefied gelatin at the edge; then remove from the bath, place a serving plate on top, and flip. ▶

▶▶ Baby mixed greens, arugula, or curly endive
Chili Cheese Flavored Fritos corn chips (or—my second choice—Fritos originals)
Dressing of choice
Margarita salt or finishing salt

▶▶ TO FINISH:

❖ Serve congealed salad slices on a bed of chopped baby mixed greens, arugula, or frisée with a small amount of dressing of your choice on the lettuce and with the corn chips as a crispy accompaniment. Sprinkle with finishing salt.

VARIATIONS

Garnish with Mexican Crema. I have also made the salad with liquid margarita mix. I simply added the liquid volumes together to get the right amount.

Chef Jennifer McKinney developed the next two recipes: the first for a Texas-style quiche and the second an all-purpose vinaigrette. (Jennifer makes the best salad dressings ever.)

¾ cup Fritos corn chips, ground into meal
¾ cup all-purpose flour
½ teaspoon baking powder
½ teaspoon salt
5 tablespoons butter, cut into small pieces
1 egg

Corn, Roasted Red Pepper, and Cheddar Quiche

By Chef Jennifer McKinney

FRITOS CRUST

❖ Pulse the dry ingredients in the food processor until they have a fine meal consistency. Pulse in the butter until the mixture resembles coarse cornmeal. Add the egg and pulse 10 more times, until the dough forms a ball. Press into a flat disk. Wrap in plastic and chill at least 1 hour.

1 ear of corn, kernels scraped
1 leek, white part only, chopped
1 tablespoon butter
3 large eggs
1 cup half-and-half
1 roasted red bell pepper
½ teaspoon salt
¼ teaspoon ground black pepper
½ cup grated Cheddar cheese

NOW MAKE THE FILLING:

❖ Sauté the corn kernels and chopped leeks in the butter until tender. Set aside. In a bowl, whisk together the eggs and half-and-half. Add the sautéed corn and leeks, the red bell pepper, and the salt and pepper. Preheat the oven to 350 degrees. Press the chilled dough into a pie pan or tart pans to form a uniform ¼-inch crust. Bake covered with foil and pie weights for 15 minutes or until firm and light golden brown. Remove from the oven. Sprinkle with half the cheddar. Pour in the filling. Sprinkle with the remaining cheddar. Bake until the custard has set, about 30 minutes.

Roasted Poblano Vinaigrette

❖ Combine all the ingredients in a blender or food processor and purée until smooth. This can be made up in advance. Keep refrigerated.

I recently taught my son Alex to make this recipe for guacamole. When my brothers and I were kids they made it after school and taught me how to make it.

2   poblano chilies, roasted, peeled, seeded, and chopped
2   tablespoons cold water
1   tablespoon red wine vinegar
1   clove garlic, chopped
1   tablespoon honey
¼   cup canola oil
1   teaspoon salt
¼   teaspoon ground black pepper

Frito Kids Guacamole (original)

❖ Cut each avocado in half lengthwise with the peel on. Twist the halves in opposite directions until they separate. Take a sharp knife and whack the seed with the knife-edge until it sticks. Twist and remove the seed on the knife. If you are not serving the guacamole immediately, then save the seeds to push down into the middle of the finished salad to help to prevent the avocados from turning brown. (This may be a folktale, but I do it anyway.) Cube the avocado while it's in the skin and scoop out onto a plate to smash with a fork. Add all the remaining ingredients and mix.

2   avocados
1   diced tomato, seeds and pulp removed
1   teaspoon garlic powder
1   tablespoon chili powder
2   tablespoons Meyer lemon juice
¼   teaspoon Pico Limon (a Mexican chili powder, ascorbic acid powder, and salt mixture)
1   very finely diced jalapeño, seeded and deveined

Mexican-inspired cuisine has come a long way since the days of the recipes described in chapter 6, "Inventors and Inventions." In the early days Tex-Mex food was called Mexican food. I have enjoyed Tex-Mex food all of my life, but it has gotten very interesting in the last several years, as gourmet chefs from America and Mexico have adapted it. The influence of chefs from Mexico, particularly from Mexico City, has also given us many new and interesting varieties of authentic Mexican cuisine.

The recipe below was given to me by Raul Delgado, who helped in my workshops at the Latino Cultural Center in Dallas. When I told him about this book he told me that he usually makes migas (Mexican scrambled eggs) with Fritos in them rather than tortilla chips.

Fritos Migas (original, adapted)

By Kaleta Doolin and Raul Delgado

❖ Oil the skillet and heat. In a small mixing bowl, whisk the eggs until they become lemon colored. Add the other ingredients. Let stand until the corn chips begin to soften. Pour the egg mixture into a hot skillet and begin stirring. (I like to stir my scrambled eggs with a spoon to make small rounded clumps.) Serves 4.

8   eggs
1   can (4 ounces) chopped Hatch chilies
3   slices jalapeño pepper jack cheese, cut into small pieces
3   tomatoes, seeded and chopped
1   cup Fritos corn chips
    Salt and pepper to taste

Chef Jennifer McKinney and I developed this recipe by taste, trying to get as close as possible to something I'd eaten in a restaurant.

Goat-Cheese-Stuffed, Fritos-Crusted Chile Relleno with Tomatillo, Pea, and Mint Sauce
(original)

By Kaleta Doolin and Chef Jennifer McKinney

This recipe involves several steps. You roast poblanos, make a batter and fill them, roll them in a special coating, deep fry them, and serve them under a minted tomatillo sauce. (You will have leftover sauce that you can use to make the next two dishes.)

4 poblano peppers
   Canola oil spray

FIRST, ROAST THE POBLANOS:

❖ Spray the peppers with canola oil. Roast them, turning to char all sides, over an open flame on a gas stove or grill, or blister (again, turning on all sides) under a high broiler in the oven. Place in a bowl and cover with foil. Allow to sit at least 10 minutes and peel. Scrape (do not use running water as the flavor is in the natural pepper oils.) Gently scrape char from peppers using a paring knife. Slit down the middle, keeping the stem intact. Remove the seeds.

1 teaspoon salt
1 teaspoon cumin
8 ounces goat cheese
1 clove garlic, minced and sautéed
1 tablespoon vegetable oil
2 tablespoons chopped shallots
¼ teaspoon dried oregano

NEXT, MAKE THE FILLING:

❖ Mix together all filling ingredients. Divide filling by four. Stuff each pepper with the filling mixture. Roll up tight.

8 tomatillos, husked
½ cup peas
¾ cup onion
2 cups vegetable broth
1 cup fresh mint leaves
   Salt and pepper to taste
   (about 1 teaspoon salt)

NOW FOR THE SAUCE:

TOMATILLO, PEA, AND MINT SAUCE

❖ Combine the tomatillos, peas, onion, and broth in a saucepan. Simmer until the onion is soft. Puree with the mint in a food processor or blender. Add salt and pepper.

½ cup flour
3 large eggs, beaten
2½ cups Fritos corn chips, lightly crushed

NOW COAT AND STUFF THE POBLANOS:

❖ Roll each filled poblano in the flour and dip it in the egg and then the crushed corn chips.

FINALLY, COOK AND SERVE THE POBLANOS:

❖ Heat the oil to 350 degrees in a deep pot. Fry the stuffed peppers, gently turning with a slotted spoon or tongs, until golden brown and crispy. Drain on paper towels. Sauce the plate and top with relleno.

3 cups vegetable oil

Hatch Pepper, Tomatillo, Pea, and Mint Dip

❖ Sauté the onions in the butter until soft. Add the remaining ingredients. Mix well. Serve hot or cold.

½ onion, chopped
1½ tablespoons butter
2 cans (4 ounces each) chopped Hatch peppers, drained
¼ cup Tomatillo, Pea, Mint Sauce (see recipe above)
1 package (16 ounces) cream cheese
1   cup sour cream
1½ tablespoons butter
1 teaspoon salt
1 teaspoon cumin, ground

Goat Cheese Chilequiles with Tomatillo Pea and Mint Sauce

❖ Roast and peel the peppers as you would for Chili Rellenos (recipe above). Cut in strips and put in an oiled casserole dish. Pinch the goat cheese into the casserole. Sprinkle the top with the corn chips, salt, and pepper. Heat until the chips turn golden and the cheese is hot. In a separate pan heat the Tomatillo, Pea, and Mint Sauce. Serve it in a gravy boat alongside plated chilaquiles servings. This is much like a variation of nachos. Makes a great lunch for 2–3 people.

4 poblano peppers
8 ounces goat cheese
Salt and pepper to taste (about I teaspoon salt)
Fritos corn chips
About 1 cup Tomatillo, Pea, and Mint Sauce (see recipe above)

I found the recipe below in a cookbook I bought in Central Market, my local grocery store. The book, called The First Ever Unedited and Untested Hatch Chile Pepper Recipe Book, *contains recipes submitted to a Hatch chili pepper recipe contest. This recipe, created by Jerry and Victoria Ayers of Arlington, Texas, was one of the winners. I modified it to include Fritos (and called the authors of the book for permission to modify it and include it here).*

1 cup quinoa
1 tablespoons toasted cumin seeds
2 + 1 cups chicken broth *or* vegetable broth
1½ pounds Hatch chilies (or use canned, peeled, chopped Hatch peppers; also called "Anaheim" chilies)
1 medium onion, chopped
6 cloves garlic, minced
4 dates, chopped
1½ cups black beans, cooked
½ cup cilantro, chopped
1 + 1 teaspoons ground cumin
½ + ½ teaspoon ground allspice
½ teaspoon ground coriander
2 cups diced tomatoes
2 teaspoons dried oregano
10 extra-large eggs
1½ cups sharp Cheddar cheese, grated
   Toasted pumpkin seeds
   Fritos corn chips, original size

Hatchin' Huevos with Fritos

By Jerry and Vicoria Ayers

❖ Stir the quinoa and toasted cumin seeds into the 2 cups of chicken broth (or vegetable broth) and bring to a boil. Reduce the heat and simmer for 15 minutes until the quinoa has absorbed the liquid. Remove from heat and let cool. If you are using fresh chilies, roast them until blistered, then cool and remove the charred skins and seeds. Coarsely chop.

Sauté the onion and garlic in a little oil until translucent. Stir in the dates, black beans, cilantro, and quinoa mixture. Cook over low heat until thoroughly heated. Remove from heat, stir in 1 teaspoon of the ground cumin, ½ teaspoon of the ground allspice, and all the ground coriander. Cover and keep warm.

Cook the tomatoes with the other cup of broth until reduced by half. Stir in all the remaining cumin, allspice, and oregano (that is, 1 teaspoon of the cumin, ½ teaspoon of the allspice, and the 2 teaspoons oregano). Keep the tomato mixture hot—but just below boiling so the oregano will not go off flavor.

MEANWHILE, SCRAMBLE THE EGGS.

❖ To assemble: Spread a generous portion of the quinoa mixture in the bottom of the casserole. Spread the scrambled eggs on top of the quinoa. Top with the chopped chilies and grated cheese and ladle on the hot tomato mixture. Sprinkle with the toasted pumpkin seeds and serve with a basket of the corn chips.

NOTES: Some sharp Cheddar cheeses do not melt very well and do not give up their oil. Ask your grocer to recommend the best for cooking. I like to serve this dish with half an avocado, sliced and sprinkled with a hint of garlic salt.

The recipe below grew out of chef Jennifer McKinney's idea of making batters using ground Fritos. Negro Modelo, a Mexican beer, brings the flavor of Mexico to this batter, which can be used for frying red snapper or other kinds of fish. Many recipes for authentic Mexican food use red snapper. Once we discovered this recipe, my family started asking for it over and over.

1 cup flour
½ cup Fritos corn chips, ground fine
1⅛ cups dark beer (a little less than a full bottle of Negro Modelo)
½ teaspoon salt
1 pound red snapper filets (or other white fish such as cod, flounder, or catfish)

Red Snapper in Negro Modelo Batter

❖ Whisk together the first four ingredients and let stand for 15 minutes. The batter should be the consistency of very soft peanut butter.

Wash and dry the fish. Fill a pan large enough for the filets with 3 inches of vegetable oil. Heat to about 370 degrees. Batter the fish, fry, and serve immediately.

The best mole I've ever tasted was made by Yolanda Cuellar, who was married to the late Mack Cuellar of the El Chico chain of Mexican restaurants in the Southwest. I'm friends with Yolanda's daughter Lupita Allen—we like to talk about how we're both daughters of food industry entrepreneur fathers. Lupita and I sometimes attend luncheons with other daughters of high-powered entrepreneurs. Yolanda's recipe for Green Chicken Mole was served at one of these luncheons. Yolanda uses only chicken thigh meat because she thinks that chicken breasts are too dry. Her cooking is more inspired by Spanish cuisine than her husband's famous Tex-Mex dishes. This recipe takes a lot of time, but it's the real thing.

Green Chicken Mole

By Yolanda Cuellar

❖ Boil the chicken with ½ of the onion and garlic. When almost cooked, pull the chicken from the broth and set both the broth and the chicken aside. Place all the remaining ingredients except the oil in a blender and blend well. In a large saucepan, heat the oil and sauté the blended ingredients for a minute. Slowly add some of the broth to make a thick gravy. Season the mixture with salt to taste, continue to simmer it for about three to four minutes, return the chicken thighs, and cook until they are done (about 10 minutes). If the gravy gets too thick add more broth.

NOTE: If you're in a hurry, Yolanda's favorite brand of green mole off the shelf is Doña Maria. You can simply boil the chicken thighs, heat the sauce and add the thighs.

6	chicken thighs
1	small onion (roughly chopped)
1	to 2 cloves garlic
1½	pounds green tomatillos
	Leaves from 2 stems epazote
½	cup unsalted peanuts
3	large romaine lettuce leaves
2	ounces pumpkin seeds
¼	cup walnuts
4	tablespoons vegetable cooking oil
	Salt to taste

Yolanda Cuellar's Rice Ring

❖ Add the salt and butter to the water and bring to a rapid boil. Immediately add the rice and black pepper and bring back to a boil. Cover and cook over low heat for 25 minutes. (The rice should be fluffy and all the water absorbed.) Spray a Bundt pan with the cooking spray. Add the sour cream, chilies, and cheese to the rice. Blend evenly and spoon the mixture into the Bundt pan. Press down gently, packing well. Preheat the oven to 350 and cook for 30–40 minutes until slightly golden on top. After removing from the oven let sit for about 8–10 minutes before turning over on a serving dish.

2½	teaspoons salt
2	tablespoons butter
4	cups water
2	cups rice
½	teaspoon black pepper
	Cooking spray, such as Pam
16	ounces sour cream
3	to 4 small cans chopped greenchilies, drained
8	ounces Monterey Jack cheese, grated

Mom and I reconstructed Mom's recipe for Fritoque Pie, which was a winner in the 1932 Frito Company recipe competition. It was a frequent dinner casserole served in our home when I was a kid. The original recipe had gotten lost over the years; hence, we had to reconstruct it—in the kitchen, feeling our way along, figuring out the ingredients and measurements, then tasting and adding until we got it right. My college Food Preparation 101 class served me well—I knew that it needed eggs to leaven it and flour to bind it, chicken broth instead of beef broth because it has turkey, and so on.

1 bag (10 ounces) Fritos corn chips, original size
4 cups cooked turkey (cut into ½-inch dice)
3 cups celery, finely diced
2 cups sweet onion, diced (one medium onion)
4 tablespoons butter to sauté the veggies + 2 tablespoons for sauce
2 tablespoons whole-wheat flour
1 cup chicken broth
4 eggs, lightly beaten

Fritoque Pie (vintage, reconstructed)

By Mary Kathryn Doolin with Kaleta Doolin

❖ Lightly crush the corn chips in their sealed bag to make about ½-inch pieces. In a large bowl, refine the texture by hand and with the back of a mixing spoon. Save 1 cup in a separate bowl for a top crust. Add the turkey to the remaining chips. Sauté the celery and onions in the butter and add to the turkey and chips. Stir. Make a roux by browning the whole-wheat flour with the melted butter. Add the chicken broth to make a medium sauce. Stir with a wire whisk until cool. Add to the turkey, vegetable, and chip mixture. Add the eggs and stir. Place in an oiled casserole pan. Cover and bake at 350 degrees for 50 minutes. Add a top crust of the remaining cup of crushed chips. Warm uncovered for another 5 minutes.

VARIATIONS

❖ Melt grated cheddar on top. Substitute chicken for the turkey. Add green peas with the chicken to make a Fritos potpie casserole.

Wesley Rankin Community Center Tamales

By Irma Gonzales Flores

This recipe makes 100 dozen tamales – that's right, 1,200 tamales.

A local community center makes this bulk recipe for tamales and sells the results as a fundraiser. Irma Flores, who shared this family recipe with me, said that her mother's first rule for cooking was that everyone in the kitchen should always wear a hairnet and an apron.

BEEF FILLING:

❖ Put the briskets into several large pots and cover with water. Blend together 12 cups ancho chili powder and 2 cups salt or if you want make a hotter tamale spice blend use a mixture of ancho (mild), pasilla (hot), and guajillo (medium to hot) dried ground peppers. Divide the mixture proportionately to the amount of meat and water in each pot. (I used 3 quarts water to 10 pounds of meat per pot.) Bring the water to a boil and then turn down to a simmer. Simmer the meat for three or four hours until very tender. Remove the meat from the broth, saving the broth to make gravy for the meat filling mixture and the masa mixture. Chill the broth in the refrigerator and skim the fat off the top. Prepare the meat by removing and discarding most of the fat (leaving about 1/8 inch of fat) and then chopping the remaining meat very fine. Make a gravy by heating 10 pounds lard in a deep pot. Add 3 cups masa harina flour, 2 cups garlic powder, 1 ½ cups cumin, and ¼ cup salt. Add 30 quarts of broth. Boil to reduce and thicken the gravy (adding more masa harina if needed), and then add 22 quarts of the gravy to the chopped meat and heat until it begins to bubble around the edges. Remove from heat. Adjust the seasonings to taste. Marylou, one of Irma's sisters who helps Irma at the community center said, "You should add salt until you can taste it in both the meat and masa mixtures."

45	quarts water
150	pounds beef brisket)about 15 briskets)
12	cups ancho chili powder (or a blend of ancho, pasilla, and guqjillo)
2	cups + ¼ cup salt
10	pounds lard
3	cups masa harina flour
2	cups garlic powder
1½	cups ground cumin

Clean the cornhusks and soak them in scalding water to soften for a minimum of two hours. (This may be done the night before, with the cornhusks left soaking overnight).

1200 large or 1260 small cornhusks

MASA:

❖ Mix salt, paprika, cumin, and garlic powder. Divide the dough and the spice mix into batches that fit into the bowl of a large heavy-duty mixer. With the mixer on low, slowly add beef gravy to make dough moist. Increase the mixer speed to medium and begin adding the lard spoonful by spoonful. Beat the mixture until the masa has a spongy light texture, at least 10 minutes. The masa is the right consistency when you spread it on your hand and it does not stick. Another test for consistency is to drop a small ball of dough in a glass of water. It is the right proportion if the ball floats.

2⅛	cups salt
5	cups paprika
⅔	cup ground cumin
1	cup garlic powder
100	pounds store-bought pre-mixed masa dough
14	pounds lard
8	quarts gravy from broth

ASSEMBLING THE TAMALES:

❖ Remove the excess water from the cornhusks. I do this by wringing small batches as I remove them from the water. Spread 2 heaping tablespoons of masa in the middle of each cornhusk wrapper. Spread evenly from edge to edge all the way to the bottom and about 4 inches high toward the top of the husk (I trimmed the husks to the size of my palm). Put 1 heaping tablespoon of meat filling in the center of each square and spread in a vertical line down the middle. Fold in the left side of the wrapper first, and then fold in the right side so that the ▶

▶▶ masa forms around the filling. Always fold the top of the husk over toward the back to keep the tamale wrappers from coming loose. (If you want to store some of the tamales, go ahead and freeze them uncooked; you can steam them later).

PREPARATION:

❖ Stand the tamales upright, envelope side down, on an elevated steamer rack in a large covered pot packed around a ball of foil placed in the middle of the rack. (My steaming rack was not a perfect fit, so I also used a long "rope" of foil coiled around and around from the bottom of the pan to the level of the elevated rack to fill in the gap between the sides of the pan and the rack in order to support the tamales which were around the outer edges). The ball of foil in the center of the tamales is used to make a vent, which helps to distribute the steam evenly. Steam for 1½ hours, replenishing the water as needed. Be sure not to let the pot boil dry, and do not let the tamales touch the water. If the pot is very wide and covers two burners, turn the pot ¼ turn every half hour to keep it heating evenly. (Irma and her sister Marylou told me that their mother always said, "Do not walk out of the house or it will ruin the whole batch!") The cooked tamales may be frozen and reheated. To reheat frozen cooked tamales, steam for 25 minutes. To cook frozen uncooked tamales, follow the preparation directions above. The Gonzales sisters say that the tamales taste the same either way.

---

1   egg white, lightly beaten
⅓   cup sugar
2   teaspoons ancho chili powder
¼   teaspoon cayenne chili powder
2   cups Fritos corn chips

Salad Topper Fritos

By Kaleta Doolin with Chef Jennifer McKinney

❖ Preheat the oven to 350 degrees. Line a baking sheet with nonstick foil. After lightly beating the egg whites, mix them together with the sugar, ancho chili powder, and cayenne powder, and dump the mixture out onto a large piece of waxed paper. Gently toss the corn chips in the egg whites to coat, put them into the sugar-and-spice mixture, and lift the sides of the wax paper to toss the mixture over the chips until they are coated. Scatter them on the cookie sheet. Bake for about 10 minutes. Remove, cool, and enjoy.

---

1   bunch Swiss chard, washed, thin ends chopped to make ½ cup and leaves torn into pieces
¾   cup finely diced sweet onion
2   tablespoons olive oil
1   clove garlic, minced ▶

Swiss Chard Gratin (original)

By Chef Jennifer McKinney

❖ Sauté the chopped Swiss chard stems and onions in the olive oil until soft. Add the garlic. Stir while sautéing for another 1–2 minutes 'til the moisture has evaporated. Add the salt, pepper, ▶

▶ ▶ red pepper flakes, and heavy cream. Allow to simmer until the liquid has reduced to a thick, creamy consistency. Stir in the ¼ cup asiago. Adjust the seasonings. Place in a shallow baking dish. Sprinkle with the 2 tablespoons asiago and crushed corn chips. Bake at 375 degrees for 20 minutes.

▶ ▶ Salt and ground black pepper
Pinch of red pepper flakes
1   cup heavy cream
¼   cup + 2 tablespoons shredded asiago cheese
½   cup finely crushed Fritos corn chips

Duck, Dried Cherry, and Ancho Tamale Tart Appetizers

By Chef Jennifer Mckinney and Kaleta Doolin

You'll need to make tamale tart shells before preparing the duck filling.

TAMALE TART SHELLS:

❖ Combine the liquefied corn chips, tamale mix, baking powder, and salt in a bowl. Add the beef broth. Work it with your fingers to make a soft, moist dough. Beat the vegetable shortening in a small bowl until fluffy, add the dough, and beat until it has a spongy texture. Press into 8 mini-tart molds. Cook over boiling water to steam the tart shells until firm. (I use a 10-inch bamboo steamer over a 10-inch pot or a small wok.)

5   ounces Fritos corn chips, liquefied in food processor
1   cup tamale mix (Maseca brand)
½   teaspoon baking powder
¼   teaspoon salt
1   cup beef broth
¼   cup chilled, hydrogenated vegetable shortening

NOW, PREPARE THE DUCK FILLING:

❖ Score the fat side of the duck breasts. Pat dry. Sprinkle all over with the salt, pepper, and half of the ancho chili powder. In a sauté pan over medium heat, render the fat from the duck breast until brown and crisp. Bake the duck breasts in a 375-degree oven for about 15 minutes or until medium-rare. Shred the duck by hand when cooled. Toss the pearl onions in olive oil and roast them in a 450-degree oven until browned. In a small saucepan, melt the sugar until light caramel brown—carefully. Add the vinegar and whisk (the liquid will boil up, so stand back). Add the roasted onions, the dried cherries with their liquid, and the other half of the ancho chili powder, the shredded duck breast and mix. Fill the tart shells with the duck mixture. Add more salt and pepper to taste. Serves 8.

2   large Muscovy duck breasts
½   teaspoon salt
¼   teaspoon black pepper
½   + ½ teaspoon ancho chili powder
1   cup pearl onions, skins removed
2   tablespoons olive oil
½   cup sugar
½   cup red wine vinegar
1   cup dried cherries (preferably sun-dried), soaked in ¾ cup hot water that has just been brought to boiling

Below are some recipes that represent my train of thought as I tried to make Molasses Pie (see chapter 10, "Desserts") into something good. In the end I only used the crust ingredient part of the Molasses Pie recipe and made a filling that I knew would make a delicious combination with the salty corn flavor of the crust—a pumpkin and squash pie. Since it was Halloween, the grocery store had many pumpkins of all sizes. The small one that I picked out had a recipe label on it. I also bought another regular-sized ▶

▶ ▶ *pumpkin. The small pumpkin turned out to be a squash, but I used it anyway since my mom has always used butternut squash instead of pumpkin in her holiday pies. I used half of the small pumpkin look-alike, and used drained pureed pumpkin for the rest of the quantity needed for the filling recipe. I steamed wedges that I cut from the real, larger pumpkin and then scooped the meat out of the skins. (Dr. Shelton, Mom and Dad's "guru," taught them—and they taught me—that most of the vitamins of vegetables are closest to the skin. Therefore, instead of peeling the pumpkin and then steaming it, I did it the Dr. Shelton way, steaming the pumpkin first and scraping the skin, scraping as hard as I could without breaking the skin.) Next I adapted the original Molasses Pie Crust by leaving out the water and the salt (since the oil in the Fritos provides enough moisture and I decided that the Fritos themselves contain enough salt.) I call this a crumb crust because of the texture the Fritos give it and because I press it into the pan like a graham cracker crumb crust.*

⅓ cup shortening
1 cup flour
1 teaspoon baking powder
1 cup Fritos corn chips, crushed

Corn Chip Crumb Crust (original)

By Kaleta Doolin

❖ Mix the shortening with the dry ingredients. Add the corn chips and mix thoroughly. Line the bottom and sides of the pie pan. Press the dough in to even out the thickness.

1 cup packed light brown sugar
1 cup granulated sugar
3 tablespoons + 1 teaspoon pumpkin pie spice (a recipe for this follows)
1½ cups fresh pumpkin puree, drained
1½ cups fresh squash puree, drained
10 ounces evaporated milk (or lowfat milk)
6 eggs, lightly beaten with a whisk
Whipped cream (add 1 tablespoon powdered sugar if you want to lightly sweeten

Pumpkin and Squash Pie Filling

This recipe yields filling for two 8-inch pies.

❖ Preheat the oven to 400 degrees. Mix the brown sugar, granulated sugar, and the 3 tablespoons of pumpkin pie spice. Stir. Mix the pumpkin puree and squash puree together, add it to the sugar mixture, and blend well. Add the milk and lightly beaten eggs. Stir until blended and smooth. Pour the mixture into Corn Chip Crumb Crust pie shells (recipe above). Bake the pies for 15 minutes. Reduce the oven temperature to 350 degrees and continue baking for another 45 minutes. Cool on a wire rack. Spoon a large dollop of whipped cream on top of each pie slice or spread evenly over the top of the pie and then slice.

¼ cup cinnamon, 4 teaspoons ground ginger, and 2 teaspoons nutmeg ▶

Pumpkin Pie Spice

Dallas Morning News, *November 28, 2007*

Vary the ingredients to suit your taste. Combine thoroughly. ▶

▶▶ *Pumpkin seeds make a great topping for a squash soup or are good by themselves as a snack. I saved the pumpkin seeds left over from my pumpkin pie and tried to make spicy roasted pumpkin seeds out of them. I discovered after I'd made them that the real recipe calls for raw, hulled pumpkin seeds. The roasted pumpkin seeds that I made tasted like dry grass—I pictured horses and cows with mouthfuls of hay, some it sticking out of their mouths—and gave me an instant stomachache. Since pumpkin seeds are almost impossible to hull by hand, I recommend buying the raw, green, hulled seeds separately from any pumpkins you buy to bake with. Believe me, you don't want to eat any hulls.*

▶▶ *or*

¼ cup cinnamon, 1 tablespoon ground ginger, 1 tablespoon nutmeg, and 1 teaspoon ground cloves
or
¼ cup cinnamon, 2 tablespoons ground ginger, 1 tablespoon nutmeg, and 1 tablespoon ground cloves

Spicy Roasted Pumpkin Seeds

❖ In a small skillet over moderately high heat, heat the oil. Add the pumpkin seeds and cook, stirring constantly, until they begin to pop, 1–2 minutes. Stir in the cumin and cayenne pepper and continue to cook and stir until fragrant, about 30 seconds. Transfer to a bowl and season with a generous pinch of kosher or coarse sea salt.

1 tablespoon olive oil
¾ cup raw, green pumpkin seeds, hulled
¾ teaspoon ground cumin
Pinch of cayenne pepper

Mom told me hundreds of times about the only candy that she and her two sisters had when they were growing up in Floresville, Texas (close to San Antonio). It was a cone of hardened brown sugar called a Piloncillo (or Pilon for short). I found this candy at Fiesta Mart (a Mexican grocery store chain that entered the Dallas market a few years ago). I wasn't tempted to buy it, but I did buy a package of Mango Picosito candy, which was next to the Piloncillo on the shelf. Mango Picosito is a salty-sweet, tart, spicy Mexican treat. After I bought it, took it home, and tasted it, I was inspired to make a candy I called Mango Frito Picosito. I came up with the name before I even invented the recipe because I liked the sound of all those "o" endings, which reminded me of Dad's name-branding. I conceived of the recipe itself as a candied dried mango and processed Frito confection. Here's my recipe, with its snappy title.

Mango Frito Picosito (original)

By Kaleta Doolin

❖ Heat together the cup of water and cup of sugar until all the sugar is melted. Boil to reduce and until thickened. In a small skillet, cook the dried mangos in this simple syrup on high heat for about 15 minutes. Drain. Process in a food processor with the remaining ingredients until the mixture begins to roll around the bowl. Shape into small balls (about the size of Peanut ▶

1 cup water
1 cup sugar
15 ounces dried mangos
2 ounces new Pinch of Salt Fritos corn chips
½ teaspoon cayenne pepper
3 tablespoons fresh lemon juice Grated zest of 1 small organic lemon
½ cup fine granulated sugar

▶ ▶ M&Ms). Roll the balls in crème brûleé sugar (see recipe below), reshape to a sphere, and then roll in the crème brûleé sugar again. Heat the coating with a culinary torch on a cookie sheet covered with nonstick foil. Cool. Turn carefully using a spatula to break the hardened sugar loose from the foil. Heat the spot on the bottom. This freezes well and is good either frozen or at room temperature.

Crème brûlée sugar is an extra-fine sugar that these days is usually sold under the name "castor sugar." You can make your own if it's not available in your area. Here's the recipe.

½ cup firmly packed light brown sugar
½ cup granulated sugar

Crème Brûlée Sugar

❖ Spread the light brown sugar on a baking sheet lined with parchment and dry it in a 200 degree oven for 40 minutes. When it is crisp and crumbly, cool to room temperature and process in a food processor along with the white sugar. This will keep indefinitely.

Here I present what is probably my most asked-for recipe. I make these cookies and take them to potlucks or give them as gifts. I firmly believe that mace is addictive for me. Every recipe that I make with mace, including the one below, gives me an insatiable appetite. This one makes me into a cookie monster.

1 cup butter, softened
1 cup brown sugar
1½ cups white sugar
1 tablespoon milk
1½ teaspoons vanilla
2 eggs, beaten
1 cup finely crushed Fritos corn chips
2½ cups oatmeal
1½ cups flour
1¼ teaspoons baking soda
1 teaspoon salt
½ teaspoon mace
1½ teaspoons cinnamon
¼ teaspoon nutmeg
⅛ teaspoon powdered cloves
4 ounces coconut
2¼ cups chocolate chips
1 cup chopped pecans

Kaleta's Frito Nuggets (original)

❖ Preheat the oven to 350 degrees. Cream together the butter, brown sugar, and white sugar. Add the milk, vanilla, and beaten eggs. Stir in the crushed corn chips and oatmeal. Sift together the flour, baking soda, salt, mace, cinnamon, nutmeg, and powdered cloves and add them, mixing thoroughly. Stir in the coconut, chocolate chips, and pecans. Drop the batter by well-rounded teaspoons onto greased cookie sheets. Bake 10 minutes at 350 degrees.

When we stopped at gas stations on car trips with the whole family, my father often paid for the gas and came back out of the office with treats. He bought butterscotch Lifesavers for himself and Mom and mixed-fruit flavor Lifesavers for us.

Using the premise that Dad's tastes were the company's guideposts, I decided to experiment with a combination of his ▶

▶ ▶ *favorite flavors. My brother Charles told me that our dad didn't like his middle name, Elmer, because of its association with a famous cartoon character, and that made me think of a title that was too good to pass up. I worked backwards from the title to come up with a new recipe using butterscotch, sesame, and Fritos, which I named "Elmer's Fudge."*

Elmer's Fudge (original)

By Kaleta Doolin

First, you'll need to make candied Fritos and toast sesame seeds.

CANDIED FRITOS FOR FUDGE:

❖ Mix the Fritos with the castor sugar in a bowl or shake them in a paper bag. Spread in a single layer around the edges of a cookie sheet (it tends to brown faster in the middle.) Put in a 500-degree oven on high broil for about one minute. Let the sugar melt, but do not let it blacken. Turn the corn chips over and melt the sugar on other side. Break the whole chips into two or three pieces.

NOW, TOAST SOME SESAME SEEDS:

❖ Put the seeds in a large skillet. Heat until they turn golden.

NOW YOU CAN MAKE THE FUDGE:

❖ Cover the bottom and sides of an 8x8-inch cake pan with nonstick aluminum foil and spread a single layer of the toasted sesame seeds over the bottom of the pan. (It is easy to get the layer too deep, in which case some seeds may not stick to the fudge.)

Place all the other ingredients except for the candied Fritos in a large microwave-safe bowl and microwave for two minutes. Stir until smooth. If the mixture is not yet smooth, microwave a little more in small increments.

Stir in the candied Fritos.

Carefully spoon the fudge mixture over the sesame seeds as evenly as possible. Be careful not to pick the seeds up off of the bottom of the pan as you spread the fudge mixture. Chill for four or more hours. (I like to put it in the freezer and eat it frozen.)

Remove from the pan, remove the foil, and cut into cubes. The sesame layer helps to keep your fingers from getting sticky. The sugar coating on the Fritos makes a barrier that keeps the Fritos from absorbing the butter in the fudge and getting soft—but just for a day. The different textures in this recipe are sumptuous, so preferably, the fudge squares should be eaten the same day. ▶

1 heaping cup of Fritos corn chips, whole
1 tablespoon castor (super-fine) sugar or homemade crème brûlée sugar (see recipe above)

¼ cup sesame seeds

¼ cup toasted sesame seeds
1 package (11 ounces) butter-scotch chips
⅔ cup sweetened condensed milk
1 tablespoon water
1 teaspoon vanilla
1 cup miniature marshmallows
¼ teaspoon salt
1 cup of the candied Fritos

▶ ▶ I was experimenting with making butterscotch fudge from scratch. Getting the mixture up to temperature was next to impossible, so I spread it in the pan. When it reached 200 degrees it became a delicious praline. The cubes were a bit weird, so I recommend spooning the mixture into patties onto a nonstick cookie sheet.

3 cups white sugar
⅛ teaspoon salt
1 teaspoon vanilla
1 teaspoon mild molasses
5 teaspoons maple syrup
4 tablespoons butter (½ stick)
1 tablespoon marshmallow fluff
⅔ cup sweetened condensed milk
½ cup toasted sesame seeds (see recipe above)
1 cup candied Fritos (see recipe above)

Sesame Pralines

❖ Cover a cookie sheet with nonstick foil. Over medium heat, boil all of the ingredients except the sesame seeds and candied Fritos until the mixture reaches 200 degrees. Stir in the sesame seeds. Continue stirring until the mixture loses its shine. Gently add the candied Fritos. Drop by spoonfuls onto the cookie sheet to cool for at least 4 hours. (I like to use the freezer and eat them frozen.) As with the previous recipe, any candy that you don't freeze should be eaten fresh, preferably the day you make it, since the sugar coating on the Fritos protects them for only one day from absorbing butter and getting soft.

Epilogue

S HORTLY AFTER Dad's death, the Frito Company board of directors and executives assembled to ceremoniously honor my father with the reading and presentation to my mother of this proclamation.

When Charles Elmer Doolin organized The Frito Company in 1932 it employed four people, making a single product, in a single make-shift plant with sales at an annual rate of about one thousand dollars. Twenty-seven years later, the company and its related enterprises had grown to include twenty-one plants in eleven states and to employ three thousand five

My dad, Charles Elmer Doolin

hundred people making and distributing Fritos, potato chips, and a number of other products throughout the nation and in foreign countries with sales at an annual rate of sixty million dollars. These simple figures themselves represent a surpassing tribute to Charles Elmer Doolin. They are the tangible evidence of his vision, courage, and faith, as well as his ability to set a course and to guide himself and others on the path to achievement. Of equal importance was the love for him by his fellow man, his employees and business associates, earned not by worldly accomplishments alone but by qualities of character.

At my local garage, the shop owner relayed the same thing to me in different words, the words of a former Frito employee, Jerry Martin who knew my dad. He said my father did not just hang the moon, but he was the moon to his employees.

My mother, too, always glorified my dad. Everyone did. But I needed to know who the real man was. So I set off to find out, and to write this book.

Nell Morris's old scrapbook had given me a compass, but

Mom, after dad's death, being presented with the company's heartfelt resolution honoring his service. She was later offered, and accepted, a place on the board.

all the while I was writing, I longed for something more—a tangible connection to the work I was doing. Then, just as I was finishing the last draft, I found a lost Viewmaster photo—it seemed to appear magically at just the right moment. There I was, five years old, and Dad was putting a chef's hat on my head and tying a red bandana around my waist. He was about to induct me into the experimental cooking that he was doing at home. Looking back now, I feel that he was handing off the torch to me at that very moment, giving me my charge to tell his story.

Dad, handing off the torch to me.

Finding that photo at that moment in my work drew me back to where it all began. Suddenly, I was able to connect it all—the creativity and humor of my grandmother, the ingenuity of my father, and the homespun wisdom of my mother—to my own life and work as an artist. ∎

Appendix 1

Recommended Reading

The first collection below consists of cookbooks that offer the bold flavors of southwestern cooking with a rustic flair. For some of them, as for this book, the perspective is historical.

For my readers who take interest in historical contexts, and in the particular subjects presented in this book, I've included the second list. It's a collection of classic treatises that guided the life and work of that successful international entrepreneur, inventor, and agricultural innovator—the man this book is really about—my father, C. E. Doolin.

My Southwest Cookbook Collection

From childhood to the present, my own cooking has grown out of my appreciation for the traditional foods of Texas, the Southwest, and the culture of neighboring Mexico. In recent years, I have celebrated my heritage through the spicy foods and pungent flavors of my origins and have leaned much from the cooking of the many friends I have made along the way. Here are some of the cookbooks that have inspired and guided me.

Corbitt, Helen L. *Helen Corbitt's Cookbook*. Boston: Houghton Mifflin, 1957.

Corbitt, Helen L. *Helen Corbitt Cooks for Company*. Boston: Houghton Mifflin, 1974.

Disbrowe, Paula. *Cowgirl Cuisine: Rustic Recipes and Cowgirl Adventures from a Texas Ranch*. New York: William Morrow, 2007.

Fearing, Dean. *The Mansion on Turtle Creek Cookbook*. New York: Weidenfeld & Nicolson, 1987.

Flay, Bobby, with Stephanie Banyas and Sally Jackson.

Mesa Grill Cookbook: Explosive Flavors from the Southwestern Kitchen. New York: Clarkson Potter, 2007.

Flay, Bobby, with Joan Schwartz. *Bold American Food: More than 200 Revolutionary Recipes.* New York: Warner, 1994.

Foose, Martha Hall. *Screen Doors and Sweet Tea: Recipes and Tales from a Southern Cook*. New York: Clarkson Potter, 2008.

Jamison, Cheryl Alters, and Bill Jamison. *Texas Home Cooking*. Boston: Harvard Common Press, 1993.

Nelson, Davia Lee, and Nikki Silva. *Hidden Kitchens: Stories, Recipes, and More from NPR's "The Kitchen Sisters."* Emmaus, Pennsylvania: Rodale, 2005.

Nelson, Davia Lee, and Nikki Silva. *Hidden Kitchens Texas—Stories, Recipes and More from the Lone Star State.* San Francisco: Blurb Publishing (print-on-demand), 2009.

Perini, Tom. *Texas Cowboy Cooking*. Buffalo Gap, Texas: Comanche Moon, 2000.

Pyles, Stephan. *New Tastes from Texas*. Dallas: Clarkson Potter, 1998.

Pyles, Stephan. *The New Texas Cuisine*. New York: Doubleday, 1993.

Sewell, Ernestine P., and Joyce Gibson Roach. *Eats: A Folk History of Texas Food*. Fort Worth: Texas Christian University Press, 1989.

Shapiro, Laura. *Something from the Oven: Reinventing Dinner in 1950's America*. New York: Penguin, 2004.

Spears, Grady, with June Naylor. *The Texas Cowboy Kitchen*. Kansas City, Missouri: Andrews McMeel, 2003.

Thompson-Anderson, Terry. *The Texas Hill Country: A Food and Wine Lover's Paradise.* Fredericksburg, Texas: Shearer, 2008.

Tolbert, Frank X. *A Bowl of Red: The Classic Natural History of Chili con Carne with Other Delectable Dishes of the Southwest.* Dallas: Taylor, 1972.

Tolbert, Frank X. *A Bowl of Red.* Foreword by Hallie Stillwell. College Station Texas: Texas A&M University Press, 1994.

Walsh, Robb. *The Tex-Mex Cookbook: A History in Recipes and Photos.* New York: Broadway, 2004.

The C. E. Doolin Collection

Here are selections from Dad's books that I found on Mom's bookshelves, long after he died. Of greatest interest to me were the ones Dad had inscribed with his name and the ones related to subjects important in the Doolin household and the Frito Company as we were growing up: health, diet and alternative medicine, personal development, and business and innovative approaches to agriculture.

Health, Diet, and Alternative Medicine

Alsaker, R. L. *Curing Diseases of Heart and Artery.* New York: Grant Publishing, 1925.

Alsaker, R. L. *Maintaining Health "The Alsaker Way."* New York: Success Magazine Corporation Publishers, 1922.

Carque, Otto. *Vital Facts About Foods: A Guide to Health and Longevity.* Los Angeles: Natural Brands, 1933.

Davis, Adelle. *Let's Eat Right to Keep Fit.* New York: Harcourt, Brace and Company, 1954.

Hay, William Howard. *A New Era.* Mount Pocono, Pennsylvania: Hay System Publications, 1933.

Loughran, John X. *90 Days to a Better Heart.* New York: Devin-Adair, 1958.

Miller, Fred D. *Open Door to Health: A Dentist Looks at Life and Nutrition.* New York: Devin-Adair, 1959.

Shelton, Herbert M. *Food Combining Made Easy.* San Antonio: Dr. Shelton's Health School, 1951.

Shelton, Herbert M. *Human Beauty: Its Culture and Hygiene.* San Antonio: Dr. Shelton's Health School, 1958.

Shelton, Herbert M. *The Hygenic System: Ortokinesiology.* San Antonio: Dr. Shelton's Health School, 1935.

Shelton, Herbert M. *The Road to Health via Natural Hygiene.* New York: Health Guild, 1958.

Shute, Evan. *Your Heart and Vitamin E.* Detroit: Cardiac Society, 1956

.

Personal Development and Business

Drueke, William F. *Drueke's Chess Primer.* Grand Rapids, Michigan: Drueke & Sons, no date.

Genstein, Edgar S. *Stock Market Profit without Forecasting.* South Orange, New Jersey: Investment Research Press, 1954.

Getting the Most out of Life: An Anthology from "The Reader's Digest." Pleasantville, New York: Reader's Digest Association, 1946.

Haddock, Frank Channing. *Power of Will.* Meriden, Connecticut: Pelton Publishing, 1920.

Hill, Napoleon. *Think and Grow Rich.* Cleveland: Ralston Publishing, 1956.

Hopkins, Claude C. *My Life in Advertising.* New York: Harper & Brothers, 1936.

Howard, Kenneth S. *The Enjoyment of Chess Problems.* South Washington Square, Philadelphia: David McKay Company, 1943.

Laird, Donald A. *Increasing Personal Efficiency.* 4th ed. New York: Harper & Brothers, 1953.

Lasker, Emanuel. *Lasker's Chess Primer.* South Washington Square, Philadelphia: David McKay Company, 1943.

Lynch, Douglas C. *Leading and Managing Men.* New York: Ronald Press, 1950.

Mahoney, Tom. *The Great Merchants.* New York: Harper & Brothers, 1947.

Peale, Norman Vincent. *The Power of Positive Thinking.* Englewood Cliffs, New Jersey: Prentice-Hall, 1955.

Reinfeld, Fred. *Chess for Amateurs: How to Improve Your Game.* South Washington Square, Philadelphia: David McKay Company, no date.

Rosenthal, Richard S. *Spanish Self-Taught: Rosenthal's Common-Sense Method of Practical Liguistics*. New York: Garden City, 1941.

Seabury, David. *The Art of Selfishness*. Garden City, New York: Halcyon House, 1937.

Small, Marvin. *How to Attain Financial Security and Self-Confidence*. New York: Simon and Schuster, 1953.

Smith, William J. *Spotlight on Labor Unions*. New York: Duell, Sloan and Pearce, 1946.

Innovative Approaches to Agriculture

Dad was undertaking a soil-amending project in May 1959 (two months before he died) to study root rot and also the uses of manure from the cattle pens.

Faulkner, Edward H. *Plowman's Folly*. New York: Grossett and Dunlap, 1943.

Faulkner, Edward H. *A Second Look*. Norman: University of Oklahoma Press, 1947.

Faulkner, Edward H. *Uneasy Money*. Norman: University of Oklahoma Press, 1946.

Fiene, F., and Saul Blumenthal. *Handbook of Food Manufacture: Formulas and Testing*. New York: Chemical Publishing, 1938.

Howard, Sir Albert. *The Soil and Health: A Study of Organic Agriculture*. New York: Devin-Adair, 1947.

Natural Hygiene

Dad recorded Cocannouer and Pfeiffer, below, when they spoke at the natural foods conventions that we attended with him as children.

Cocannouer, Joseph A. *Weeds: Guardians of the Soil*. New York: Devin-Adair, 1954.

Natural Foods and Farming Digest. Number 1. Atlanta, Texas: Natural Food Associates, 1957.

Natural Foods and Farming Digest. Number 2. Atlanta, Texas: Natural Food Associates, 1958.

Pfeiffer, Ehrenfried, *The Earth's Faces and Human Destiny: Landscape and Its Relation to the Health of the Soil*. Emmaus, Pennsylvania: Rodale, 1947.

Rodale, J. I. *Paydirt: Farming and Gardening with Composts*. New York: Devin-Adair, 1945.

Shewell-Cooper, W. E. *The A.B.C. of the Greenhouse*. London: English Universities Press, 1951.

Appendix 2

Timelines

In the first timeline, you can see how the Frito Company grew from the time Dad bought the converted potato ricer and the 19 accounts until his death in 1959. By that time the company had bought back its franchises and had locations across the United States, except for the southeast territory held by the H. W. Lay Company.

A second timeline details some important mergers from 1959 to 1975.

The third timeline starts much later. It brings the Fritos history full circle, back to Dad's original interest in whole and healthy foods. It shows the shift back to natural foods that PepsiCo, the parent company for Fritos today, began in the 1990s.

The Frito Company during Dad's Lifetime: 1932–1959

1932
C. E. Doolin buys the recipe for Fritos from Mr. Gustavo Olguin along with 19 accounts.
Frito Company is chartered—September.

1933
Mr. and Mrs. C. E. Doolin move to Dallas.
The fifteen-cent family size bag is introduced.
Houston plant begins operation.

1934
Tulsa plant begins operation.
Fritatoes potato chip production begins.

1935
The first printed recipe, Fritos Turkey Dressing, is published and distributed on displays in stores.
First Fritos recipe folder is printed—a small folder with cartoons.
One dollar is paid to each Texas housewife sending in a new and different recipe to the Frito Company. (One account says that 19 one-dollar prizes were given to housewives who submitted winning recipes.)

1936
"Recipes of Delightful Dishes You Can Make with Fritos" is published—a small, one-color folder interspersed with cartoons about eating Fritos.
Fritos Company has a booth at the Texas Centennial.

1937
Point of Sale Department creates "Cooking with Fritos" material highlighting Fritos Turkey Dressing.
The peanut plant producing Efsees peanut butter sandwiches and Fritos Peanuts begins operations at 1411 North Haskell in Dallas (later locations are San Jacinto Street, Peak Street, and Main Street).

1938
The Fritos Company has a booth at the Pan American Exposition.
Holiday recipe folders are placed in rack headers fitted with pockets so that housewives can pick up recipes at the rack when they buy Fritos.
Research department begins in Dallas at the North Haskell plant.

1939

Six Satisfying Selections Prepared with Friendly Fritos, a larger and more colorful book, is published

The Texas Restaurant Association holds its convention in San Antonio. The Frito Company hosts this convention and serves a dinner made with Fritos.

Fluffs pork skins manufacturing begins at the North Haskell plant.

1940

C. B. Doolin (my grandfather), chairman of the board of the Frito Company, dies—January 28; Daisy Dean Doolin (my grandmother) becomes the new chairman.

1941

A special "Bride's Number" issue of the *Frito Bandwagon* features the new *Fritos Book of Recipes: Your Friendly Food Companion for Any Dish or Drink Anytime Anywhere.*
Frito Company Western Division forms —February.

For the first time, the company participates in the National School Cafeteria Convention; from a little red schoolhouse booth it hands out food value charts and copies of the *Fritos Book of Recipes*—November.

The Fritos National Company forms to create franchises.

Los Angeles plant begins operation.

1945

Promotion is curtailed until 1945 because of rationing associated with the war. Fritos Turkey Dressing is still promoted at holidays and the *Fritos Book of Recipes* is still promoted through heavy newspaper and radio ads: "Wartime snacks with Fritos" is a wartime theme.

Rack cards advertise a "happy housewife" balancing ration books with Frito recipe books.

Mary Livingston, office manager, begins experimenting with recipes from the *Fritos Book of Recipes* and promoting "Cooking with Fritos" as a substantial part of Fritos marketing.

A separate company, the Frito Sales Company, forms.

1946

Six franchises are granted to H. W. Lay & Company for locations across the United States:
1. Atlanta, Georgia
2. St. Louis, Missouri
3. Southern Ohio
4. Bethesda, Maryland
5. Monroe, Wisconsin
6. Barberton, Ohio (servicing Cleveland and Akron)

The Research Lab moves to Los Angeles

1947

Plants open across the United States and beyond:
Fritos Hawaii, Ltd., Honolulu (before Hawaii was a state—the first international plant)
Fritos Columbus
Fritos West Virginia
Fritos New York
New England Frito Corporation
Fritos Midwest (Nebraska)
Fritos Tri-State
Potato Specialty Company (Denver plant begins exclusive Tatoes operation.)
Fritos recipes appear on Fritos bags.
"Recipes and Menus for All Occasions," the first four-color recipe pamphlet is published (32 pages)—November.
"Cooking with Fritos" ad is published in *Life* magazine—December 15.

1948

1948 Recipes and Menus: America's Favorite Taste Thrill, a four-color recipe booklet, is published.
The plant in Amarillo, Texas, begins operation.
The plant in the Great Plains region begins operation.

The first marketing campaign for schools, cafeterias, hospitals, and other groups that cook in quantity is launched to encourage use of Fritos in their dishes.

Another Cooking with Fritos ad published is in *Life* magazine—January 28.

Arnold Shaw of the company's newly created Public Relations Department and Miss Livingston attend the National Education Association convention in Cleveland and the School Food Service Association convention in Detroit.

Miss Nell Morris, head dietician of Texas State College for Women in Denton, begins a program at the school to develop Fritos quantity recipes. Students work on the recipes as class projects and test over-the-counter in the school cafeteria.

National two-color advertising of "Cooking With Fritos" appears in *Life, Ladies Home Journal, Better Homes and Gardens,* and the *Christian Science Monitor;* the campaign continues into 1949.

1949

The first packet of quantity recipes is issued to district sales managers for use on their routes.

Cheetos production begins in the Dallas, Los Angeles, and Salt Lake plants.

Company-sponsored "Cook with Fritos" dinners are held in Fort Worth, Dallas, Houston, and Saint Paul, Minnesota.

The Fritos Midwest Office conducts the first practical demonstration of Fritos recipes in Omaha, Nebraska for dieticians, school cafeteria managers, food editors, and teachers.

1950

Fritos Consumer Service forms with Miss Nell Morris as director.

1951

Mail Order Department is established as part of the Frito Sales Company.

1952

The Frito Company purchases Champion Chili; Champion Chili moves to an ultramodern plant on Nagle Street in Dallas.

1953

Frito Company preferred stock is first issued— March 31.

Daisy Dean Doolin, chairman emeritus of the Frito Company, dies—September 2.

1954

The Texas Dietetic Association holds its annual meeting at the Baker Hotel in Dallas.

1959

C. E. Doolin, Fritos Company founder and chairman of the board, dies—July 22.

Enter Frito-Lay; Nell Morris Stays On: 1961–1975

1961

The Frito Company merges with the Lay Company.

1965

Doritos are introduced.

Frito-Lay merges with Pepsi-Cola becoming PepsiCo

1971

Nell Morris retires.

Pepsico's Shift toward Natural Products, 1996–2007

1996

Roger Enrico becomes CEO of PepsiCo and turns the company toward more healthful beverages.

1997

PepsiCo acquires Aquafina.

1998

PepsiCo acquires Tropicana.

2000

PepsiCo buys majority stock in Sobe.

2001

PepsiCo acquires Quaker Oats.

2002

Frito-Lay announces removal of trans fats from Doritos, Tostitos, and Cheetos.

2005

Gatorade introduces Propel Calcium.

2006

Indra Nooyi becomes CEO of PepsiCo; the company purchases Izze sparkling juice drinks.

2007

PepsiCo acquires Naked Juice.

2008

Frito-Lay launches True North (nut clusters, nut crisps, and whole nuts).

Appendix 3

Letter from C. E. Doolin to the *Frito Bandwagon*

This document, written by my father, was submitted to the editors of the *Frito Bandwagon* on the occasion of the company's twenty-fifth anniversary.

PRELUDE TO THE FRITO BUSINESS
[I] operated what was known as Highland Park Confectionery at the corner of Roseborough and Hackberry Streets in San Antonio, Texas, between the years of 1929 and 1932. Potato chips were merchandised by the manufacturers through the use of glass jars sitting on counters, and even at that date, [I] began to have ideas about merchandising bagged merchandise on display racks—but this was against the custom and on mentioning it to [my] potato chip supplier, [I] was told that the jars prevented the stealing of the merchandise in that the lid rattled when a customer would take the lid off to get the bag of potato chips. A product came into the market about 1930 called Tony's Toasted Tortillas. This product had a very good taste, being a salted, triangular type chip made from cutting tortillas into pie-shaped pieces and frying them. [I approached] the operator of the business . . . with a view to getting into the business with him. [I] was told that it was impossible to make a profit because of the stale problem, so the idea was dropped—at least temporarily. Highland Park Confectionery's principal business was ice cream of a good quality. In 1930 and 1931 the manufacturers, who were principally Mistletoe Ice Cream Company and Dairyland, got involved in a price war and the prices and the quality were dropped until the market was completely gone for quality merchandise. This was coupled with general economic conditions caused by the Depression, of course. My own business got in very bad financial shape before I gave up the idea that people would still continue to buy quality products. It was at this point that a decision had to be made. One thing was pretty evident, and that was that I was going to have to close up my confectionery. There were some personal problems too in my immediate family which did not contribute to the peace of mind necessary at that time, and I was seriously contemplating taking a job with a popsicle corporation in Houston, Texas. I ran across a product in one of my wholesale ice cream accounts that had the tenderness of the present Frito product and the taste of the toasted tortilla. The result of this find culminated in a deal with the owner of the business, who was trying to get money together to go back to Mexico. The deal involved a total of $100. With it came 19 customers, the recipe and the crude equipment that he had. Twenty dollars of the $100 was borrowed from a friend of the owner of the business, and I later learned that this friend owned a half interest at the time. He was paid back shortly after I began operating the Frito business, but it was a number of years later before I learned that he had been half-owner and had sold out with Mr. Olguin. Basically this is how the Frito business was started originally, or how it all began. The remaining part of this article is substantially correct as it is written to appear in the 25th anniversary issue. I would appreciate it greatly if you would take enough excerpts from what I have dictated here so that we can at least straighten out for the record and for the future the true story of how Fritos began.

—C.E.D. June 26, 1957

Appendix 4

Doolin Family and Frito Company Patents

Charles Bernard Doolin (my grandfather)

      1,261,495—Liquid measure and strainer—April 21, 1918

      1,311,857—Laminated fabric for tire casings—July 29, 1919

      1,696,079—Measuring and dispensing receptacle—December 18, 1928

Earl Bernard Doolin (my uncle)

      2,477,968—Package sealing machine—August 2, 1949

      2,514,479—Process of preventing rancidity of cooking fats—July 11, 1950

      2,525,213—Cooking apparatus—October 10, 1950

      2,692,630—Hogskin cutting die—October 26, 1954

      Also—1,893,570; 2,013,147; 2,116,386

Uncle Earl and Wid Gunderson (Frito engineer) jointly

      2,400,058—Racks and display devices with clip-and-bracket locking device

      —September 1950

Charles Elmer Doolin (my father)

      1,833,829—Car service tray—November 24, 1931 (My grandfather had tried to patent one of

         these but failed; Dad revamped that original and got the patent.)

      1,954,443—Dough dispensing and cutting device—April 10, 1934

      2,002,053—Corn product and method of making it—May 21, 1935

      2,907,268—Shaping and cooking machines (Ta-Cups)—October 6, 1959

Wid Gunderson and others

      436,600,777

      1,925,202

      466,932

      776,549

      1,491,286

      1,647,678

      2,137,657

      2,234,624

Recipes by Chapter

Chapter 1

Fritos Fruitcake (vintage)

Chapter 2

Frito-Ketts (Fritos' variation on the salmon
  croquette; vintage)

Fritos Happy Landings (vintage)

Fritos Eggplant Casserole (vintage)

Tuna Hors d'Oeuvre à la Frito (vintage)

Chicken con Fritos (vintage)

Fritos Corn Chip Dressing (vintage)

Fritos Fruit Salad Mold (vintage)

Fritos-Covered Ice Cream with Fritos Macaroons
  (vintage)

Fritos Macaroons (vintage)

Crispy Semi-Sweet Pie (vintage)

Fritos Thanksgiving Chicken (vintage)

Fritos Corn Chip Dressing for 50 (vintage)

Hot Pimento-Cheese Dip (vintage)

Fritos Smoke-Flavored Sardine Spread (vintage)

Snowcap Spread (vintage)

Ocean Spray's Cranberry Kitchen Cranberry
  Burrs (vintage)

Texas Sombreros (vintage)

Valentine Dainties (vintage)

Fritos Avocado Cheese Dip (vintage)

Fritocado Sandwich 1 (vintage)

Fritocado Sandwich 2 (vintage)

Calavo Dip with Heinz Salad Cream and Onion
  Soup (vintage; modified)

Calavo Dip with Heinz Salad Cream (vintage,
  modified)

Calavo Dip (vintage)

Chapter 3

Fritos Texas Loaf (vintage)

Beef-Ole (vintage)

Fritos Liver Loaf (vintage)

Miss Ferne's Chili (vintage)

Miss Ferne's Rio Vista Enchiladas (vintage)

Fritos Peanut Butter Spread (vintage)

Fritos Pimento-Cheese Spread (vintage)

Fritos Olive Butter and Cheese Spread (vintage)

Chapter 4

Green Bean Casserole with Potato Chips
  (vintage)

Squash and Onion Casserole (vintage)

Chick'n Pretzel Pie (vintage)

Pretzel Meat Loaf (vintage)

Hearty Bean Casserole (vintage)

Beef Casserole (vintage)

Aztec Casserole (vintage)

Fritos Tamale Loaf (vintage)

Tamale Royal (also called Fritos Tamale-Adas)
  (vintage)

Fritos Enchiladas (vintage)

Chapter 5

Fritos Crackling Bread (vintage)

Spoon Bread

Corn Pudding

Roquefort Dip (vintage)

Fritos Blue Cheese Dip (vintage)

Fritos Cheese Dip (also called "Fritos Philly Dip"
  (vintage)

Fritos Clam-Cheese Dip (vintage)

Appendix 6

Web Sites

To hear recordings of the voices of my mom, my dad, Dr. Shelton, and me,
check these out:

> *http://www.kitchensisters.org/hktexas/hk_texas_stories.htm*
> *http://www.npr.org/search/index.php?searchinput=The+Birth+of+the+Frito*

To learn more about Nell Morris, I found this definitive source:

> *http://www.twu.edu/library/cookbook-collection.asp*

To learn more about me and my work, visit:

> *http://www.kaleta.com*

Index

Page numbers in *italics* refer to illustrations.